ABSTRACT

Since late 2009, most offensive cyber capabilities have been unavailable to the Joint Force Commander. Outside of the boundaries of a theater of war, offensive cyber activities are limited to those in response to Presidential direction only. This limitation is a result of competing interests within the U.S. Government for control of cyberspace as an operational domain. The competition is currently being played out through an artificial legal debate over authorities and terminology.

To remove some of the subjectivity associated with the debate over cyberspace control, the author first engages in a plain language review of Congressional oversight pertaining to covert actions versus military special operations. Given the current attempts to apply this construct to cyberspace, what follows is analysis and explanation of why this approach is inappropriate for cyberspace as a domain of war. Finally, the author provides recommendations to enable a fully functional U.S. Cyber Command through executive policy, legislation, and extensive education and training for the Department of Defense workforce on cyberspace. In doing so, offensive cyber capabilities will once again be available for incorporation within campaign and contingency plans in support of the assigned mission.

ACKNOWLEDGEMENTS

For their varied assistance through all phases of my attendance at the Joint Advanced Warfighting School, I would like to take this opportunity to acknowledge:

- The entire JAWS and extended JFSC faculty, who rekindled an atrophied interest in history, forced me to look a bit beyond my engineer-biased realist view of the world, and reacquainted me with the benefits gained from planning even if one never executes the plan…

- Dr. Robert Antis, faculty mentor and thesis advisor, who calmed my dread over the whole thesis process and gave me the latitude to insert some personality into what are often very rigid and controlled academic formats and standards.

- John J. Mulligan, senior mentor extraordinaire, who sent me to JAWS in the first place (I have not yet forgiven him for that!), and for his continuous teaching by example – reminding me that the English language is an art form to be appreciated, even if one is barely capable of "See Spot. See Spot run."

- The Staff of the Ike Skelton Library, Joint Forces Staff College, for their guidance, direction, and assistance with all of the ways and means of modern academic research, none of which existed when I last spent any time in a collegiate library: Gail N., Dawn J., Jeannemarie S., Jason G., Catrina W., and Kari A. Yes, Gail, I have burned my copy of *Research Papers for Dummies*…

- All those who read through assorted chunks and drafts of this document (some multiple times!) to help with clarity of detail and flow in order to avoid miring down the reader in the acronyms and legal gobbledy-gook: Greg T., Kelly M., Doc D., and especially my Dad.

Finally, the JAWS Class of 2012-2013:

- The military members, for their friendship, patience, and good humor whilst educating this civilian on many of the finer points of a career spent in uniform on both sides of the pond. You will forever have my deepest respect and heartfelt gratitude for your service and sacrifice for our respective nations. God Speed.

- The "Civilian Cabal," for the sharing, cooperation, and occasional "Huh?" moments as we collectively navigated our way through Joint Professional *Military* Education (JPME-II) in the face of imminent fiscal crises and other unsettling events on the world stage. It has been a most interesting year.

TABLE OF CONTENTS

CHAPTER 1: INTRODUCTION

"Cyberspace... The final frontier..."[1]

Cyberspace is the most recently identified domain in the lexicon of the U.S. government (USG).[2] Unfortunately, it is also the least understood and least well codified. As with any technological advancement, it takes time for the warfighter to engage, understand inherently the benefits and risks, and recognize potential applications beyond the original intent. The Internet was originally a way for researchers to share information without having to resort to hand-carrying pounds of magnetic computer tapes from one place to another.[3] Since that first "hey, could I get a copy of that data?" the expansion has been exponential. Like the commercial world, the USG has been using cyberspace for global telecommunications, record keeping and databasing, morale and welfare activities, and command and control systems.[4] Unlike the commercial world, the USG must look beyond the mere use of the cyber domain to understanding how to wage war within it – to "let slip the dogs of war."[5]

With much false or misleading information available to the average user, cyberspace might be considered a dangerous place in which to operate: one does not often encounter fake waves while at sea, nor malicious rocks or trees on the land.

---

[1] With greatest respect and admiration for Gene Roddenberry, the creator of *Star Trek*.

[2] U.S. Joint Chiefs of Staff, *Department of Defense Dictionary of Military and Associated Terms*, Joint Publication 1-02 (Washington, DC: Joint Chiefs of Staff, 2010), s.v. "cyberspace." "A global domain within the information environment consisting of the interdependent network of information technology infrastructures, including the Internet, telecommunications networks, computer systems, and embedded processors and controllers."

[3] Gregory Gromov, "Roads and Crossroads of the Internet History," http://www.netvalley.com/history_of_internet.html (accessed 31 December 2012).

[4] U.S. Department of Defense, *Department of Defense Strategy for Operating in Cyberspace* (Washington, DC: Department of Defense, 2011), 1.

[5] William Shakespeare, *Julius Caesar*, 3.1.173.

Cyberspace has more hazards to navigation and operation than do the physical domains for one major reason: cyberspace is a man-made domain, one that has physical components such as computers and fiber optic lines but has no de facto physical substance. Cyberspace does not obey Newtonian laws of physics such as gravity, force, and equal and opposite reaction. Unlike the physical world where freak mutations of nature usually do not survive, cyberspace allows for and even encourages anachronisms and disarrangements, with nothing to correct or smooth the order of things but for active involvement on the part of the observer-participant, and even that is usually limited in extent.[6]

So why should one care? As mentioned above, the USG is a participant in cyberspace on a massive scale; if the Internet and/or cyberspace were to disappear tomorrow, the USG would be challenged to reconstitute even basic real-time communications. In a world where the command and control of nuclear weaponry is dependent primarily upon modern telecommunications, this thought is rather chilling. As such, the USG's freedom of access to and ability to operate within cyberspace must be considered a national security interest; in fact, protecting against ". . . threats, such as those that target our reliance on space and cyberspace" is listed in the *National Security Strategy* as a top priority.[7] Indeed, the defense and security of cyberspace are cited prominently in all national, departmental, and military strategies and doctrinal documents of recent years,[8] including several focused entirely on cyberspace.[9] Since cyberspace is a

---

[6] Betsy Book, "Virtual Worlds Review," http://www.virtualworldsreview.com/info/whatis.shtml (accessed 31 December 2012).

[7] U.S. President, *National Security Strategy of the United States* (Washington, DC: The White House, 2010), 4, 17.

[8] Ibid, 17-18, 27-28; U.S. Secretary of Defense, *National Defense Strategy of the United States* (Washington, DC: Department of Defense, 2008), 7; U.S. Secretary of Defense, *Sustaining U.S. Global Leadership: Priorities for 21st Century Defense* (Washington, DC: Department of Defense, 2012), 4-5;

national interest of the United States, requiring significant defense and support activities, one may infer that cyberspace is also a significant factor in the national or organizational interests for much of the rest of the world. Given the assumption that cyberspace is a necessary component for a potential adversary, it must be considered a critical requirement of that adversary. The USG should be prepared to exploit or attack that critical requirement to ensure a positive outcome in the USG's favor.[10]

Attack and exploitation are by definition offensive activities of warfighting.[11] For cyberspace to be properly defended and contested as a domain it must be viewed as an operational environment in a similar manner as are air, land, sea, and space. Cyberspace needs forces trained to operate within it, tools to aid those forces, doctrine for the use and application of offensive force, and an organizational center to consolidate all of these facets for the military and the rest of the Department of Defense (DOD). In addition to instructions, guides, and a lexicon, there needs to be a clear understanding of the strategic, operational, and tactical responsibilities of the various groups operating within the domain. An additional requirement is for a universal understanding of the rules of the road – the domestic and international laws and the governmental authorities that both allow and limit actions on behalf of the USG. For the military, this means clear

---

U.S. Joint Chiefs of Staff, *The National Military Strategy of the United States of America* (Washington, DC: Joint Chiefs of Staff, 2011), 7-8.

[9] U.S. President, *International Strategy for Cyberspace* (Washington, DC: The White House, 2011), 3; U.S. Department of Defense, *Department of Defense Strategy for Operating in Cyberspace* (Washington, DC: Department of Defense, 2011), 1-2; U.S. President, *Comprehensive National Cybersecurity Initiative - Unclassified Synopsis* (Washington, DC: The White House, 2010), 1-2.

[10] Joseph L. Strange and Richard Iron, "Center of Gravity: What Clausewitz Really Meant," *Joint Force Quarterly: JFQ* 35 (October 2004): 20-21; Joe Strange, "Centers of Gravity & Critical Vulnerabilities: Building on the Clausewitzian Foundation So That We Can All Speak the Same Language," *Perspectives on Warfighting* 4, 2nd ed. (1996): 48.

[11] *Webster's Third New International Dictionary of the English Language - Unabridged*, s.v. "attack;" U.S. Joint Chiefs of Staff, *Department of Defense Dictionary*, s.v. "exploitation."

authorities under the Code of Laws of the United States of America (aka United States Code, or USC), in accordance with all national policies and strategies.

The USG cyber community is populated by many who do not "get" cyberspace; they do not truly comprehend the complexity of the domain or the implications or repercussions of indiscriminate action therein. Those who do "get it" understand it so well as to manipulate language to argue highly subjective positions in support of their own organizational goals, especially for funding and personnel but mostly for control. They often intentionally omit explanations that might clarify the debate for those not as well versed in the subject. There is a multitude of publicly available works, both scholarly and strictly opinionated, arguing that offensive cyberspace operations fall into one of two inadequately or incorrectly characterized pigeonholes, either covert action or military activity.[12] The most enduring sticking point in the debate is the question whether offensive cyberspace operations constitute covert action as defined under U.S. law.[13] The existing legal framework for unacknowledged operations (covert action) contains a significant amount of undefined or mal-defined gray area between the authorities contained within the USC under Title 10 (Armed Forces) and those of Title 50 (War and National Defense) leading to the debate as to who should be in control of the aforementioned offensive cyberspace activities.

---

[12] Many in the legal community are debating the appropriate categorization of cyberspace, and most are using a long-standing Title 10 versus Title 50 debate as a place from which to begin their argument: Andru E. Wall, "Demystifying the Title 10-Title 50 Debate: Distinguishing Military Operations, Intelligence Activities & Covert Action," *Harvard National Security Journal* 3, no. 1 (September 2011); Joseph B. Berger III, "Covert Action: Title 10, Title 50, and the Chain of Command," *Joint Force Quarterly: JFQ* 67 (4th Quarter 2012); David Graham, "Cyber Threats and the Law of War," *Journal of National Security Law & Policy* 4, no. 1 (2010); Erik M. Mudrinich, "Cyber 3.0: The Department of Defense Strategy for Operating in Cyberspace and the Attribution Problem," *Air Force Law Review* 68 (2012); Matthew C. Waxman, "Cyber-Attacks and the use of Force: Back to the Future of Article 2(4)," *The Yale Journal of International Law* 36, no. 2 (2011).
[13] 50 USC § 413b(e).

This gamesmanship and the concomitant legal wrangling regarding who should have primacy for USG offensive actions in cyberspace have brought military offensive operations in cyberspace to a virtual standstill. Of special significance is the fact that there exists an on-going legal interpretational debate as to whether the military should even *have* the ability to execute offensive activities in cyberspace. For the joint force commander, this would mean that the full spectrum of military operations would not be available to support the command's mission.

In order to develop an effective and fully functional U.S. Cyber Command (USCYBERCOM), which includes Title 10 offensive authorities and capabilities, specific policy, legal, and legislative procedural actions must be implemented. The research and analysis herein will show that the legal authorities for cyberspace cannot be forced into either of the inadequate pigeonholes, and will provide a possible way ahead towards the creation of a new hole for this domain. The objective is to remove much of the mystery, bias, ignorance, and fog involved in the operational cyberspace debate and to present a clear outline for the necessary steps towards resolution of the current standstill. The suggested resolution will permit USCYBERCOM to execute offensive operations in cyberspace in support of U.S. Government objectives, to include those of a joint force commander during military operations.

Law is the Heart of the Matter

While cyberspace technology, capabilities, and user counts have exploded over the last two decades, the law has largely failed to keep up. Every day there are stories of website defacement, on-line service denial, identity theft, intellectual property exploitation, and more.[14] Around each corner, there is someone on a soapbox decrying

how poorly cyberspace is defended, and that a "cyber 9/11" or "cyber Pearl Harbor" is

imminent.[15] In all fairness to the legal community, failing to keep up with technology is

not unique to cyberspace: when the automobile first arrived on the scene, it took time for

the populace to decide that rules might be necessary to guide the use of this new device,

and then to enact those rules accordingly.[16] It is human nature to seize upon a new tool

or capability, learn through trial and error that there may be limits to how one may use

the tool safely, and that there might be malicious uses of that tool which law-abiding

citizens would never have imagined at the outset. The law is nearly always in a reactive

mode: defenses are built in after someone points out vulnerability, where 'someone' is

often a bad actor. Laws to deter those who would exploit the vulnerability are enacted in

the same after-the-fact manner.

Law enforcement is made difficult by the need for accurate attribution, both in the

physical world and in cyberspace. A pimply-faced teenager with too much time on his

hands, sitting in his parents' basement somewhere in Middle America, can masquerade

---

[14] David Goldman, "Major Banks Hit with Biggest Cyberattacks in History," *CNN Money,* 28 September 2012, http://money.cnn.com/2012/09/27/technology/bank-cyberattacks/index.html (accessed 18 January 2013); Bob Violino, "How to Stop Your Executive from being Harpooned," *Infoworld,* 23 May 2011, http://www.infoworld.com/d/security/how-stop-your-executives-being-harpooned-946 (accessed 18 January 2013); "Marching Off to Cyberwar," *The Economist Technology Quarterly* (Q4 2008).

[15] Eric Engleman and Michael Riley, "Political Gridlock Leaves U.S. Facing Cyber Pearl Harbor," *Bloomberg,* 15 November 2012; Mark Clayton, "'Cyber Pearl Harbor': Could Future Cyberattack really be that Devastating?" *The Christian Science Monitor,* 07 December 2012, http://www.csmonitor.com/USA/2012/1207/Cyber-Pearl-Harbor-Could-future-cyberattack-really-be-that-devastating (accessed 12 January 2013); Elisabeth Bumiller and Thom Shanker, "Panetta Warns of Dire Threat of Cyberattack on U.S." *New York Times,* 11 October 2012; Stacy Cowley, "Former FBI Cyber Cop Worries about a Digital 9/11," *CNN Money,* 25 July 2012, http://money.cnn.com/2012/07/25/technology/blackhat-shawn-henry/index.htm (accessed 12 January 2013); Cynthia Hodges, "United States Official Warned of 'Cyber 9/11' Threat," *Examiner.Com,* 03 December 2012, http://www.examiner.com/article/united-states-officials-warned-of-cyber-9-11-threat (accessed 12 January 2013).

[16] Randy Alfred, "May 21, 1901: Connecticut Sets First Speed Limit at 12 MPH," *Wired.Com,* 21 May 2008, http://www.wired.com/science/discoveview/news/2008/05/dayintech_0521 (accessed 02 January 2013).

on-line as anyone from anywhere he would like to be. He does this by using simple tools he can find via a little bit of research on the Internet. He may then turn around and attempt malicious harm to the Internet or its users by applying other tools he found during his research.[17] Multiply that by hundreds or thousands of individuals per day: the volume is staggering, and the burden of proof is on the cyber crime prevention and prosecution community.

To make matters more difficult for law enforcement, the user community of the Internet often leaves itself wide open to the criminal element, just as it does in the real world. Individuals fail to implement security out of ignorance of the risk or a lack of knowledge on how to protect themselves; corporations and governments avoid implementing network security because of the bottom line as well as ignorance. Cyberspace security is difficult to do well with a high degree of assurance and will be costly when done right. Companies have allowed their intellectual property to be stolen via cyberspace because it would cost more to apply security protection measures to their networks than they might lose in business profits as a result of bad actors pirating their equipment or services.[18]

---

[17] Mat Honan, "Cosmo, the Hacker 'God' Who Fell to Earth," *Wired,* 11 September 2012; Andre Yoskowitz, "Teenage Hacker Arrested for Hitting 259 Websites," *AfterDawn News,* 20 April 2012, http://www.afterdawn.com/news/article.cfm/2012/04/20/teenage_hacker_arrested_for_hitting_259_website s (accessed 2 January 2013); GMA News, "Teenage Hackers Arrested for Hit on UK Police's Anti-Terror Hotline," *GMA News Online,* 15 April 2012, http://www.gmanetwork.com/news/story/255022/scitech/technology/teenage-hackers-arrested-for-hit-on-uk-police-s-anti-terror-hotline (accessed 2 January 2013).

[18] Jen Lin-Liu, "Huawei-Cisco Tests China's Respect for Property Rights," *IEEE Spectrum,* August 2003; Stew Magnuson, "Defense Department Partners with Industry to Stem Staggering Cybertheft Losses," *National Defense,* December 2011; Dean Takaheshi, "Intellectual Property Theft Fuels Underground Cyber Economy," *Venture Beat,* 27 March 2011, http://venturebeat.com/2011/03/27/intellectual-property-theft-fuels-the-underground-cyber-economy/ (accessed 18 January 2013); Scott Berinato, "Calculated Risk: Return on Security Investment," *CSO: Security and Risk,* 09 December 2002, http://www.csoonline.com/article/217727/calculated-risk-return-on-security-investment (accessed 18 January 2013).

In the United States, a number of utilities, networks (banking, air traffic control, etc.), and other capabilities have been designated as *critical infrastructure* (CI).[19] Securing this CI will be a challenge: most is privately vice publicly owned, and there is limited incentive for the owner-operators to make major efforts to secure it absent an actual damaging event, after which it will be too late (closing the proverbial barn door after the livestock has departed). Unless and until the USG directs via law that it be done, industry will continue to balk. Several recent congressional efforts to set some initial criteria and guidance for cyber security of critical infrastructures have tried and thus far failed.[20] Public statements on the inability of Congress and industry to come to reasonable initial agreement vary. No resolution will come about until the USG is prepared to either pay for part or all of the security or accept the political fallout following the increased costs levied on the users by industry. It is not in the nature of business to do something this difficult and costly out of the goodness of their hearts. In addition to the cost implications, any legislation must be very specific to avoid loopholes and liability questions. Details must include what has to be protected (an entire CI network or only the gateways to the public Internet); what security standards will be required; who will determine those standards and set criteria for implementation; who

---

[19] U.S. President, Presidential Decision Directive, "Critical Infrastructure Protection," PDD-63 (Washington, DC: The White House, 1998); and U.S. President, Homeland Security Presidential Directive, "Critical Infrastructure Identification, Prioritization, and Protection," HSPD-7 (Washington, DC: The White House, 2003). PDD-63 recognized certain parts of the national infrastructure as critical to the national and economic security of the United States and the well-being of its citizenry, and required steps be taken to protect it. HSPD-7 established a national policy for Federal departments and agencies to identify and prioritize critical infrastructure and to protect them from terrorist attacks. The directive defined relevant terms and delivered 31 policy statements. These policy statements defined what the directive covers and the roles various federal, state, and local agencies will play in carrying them out.

[20] *Strengthening and Enhancing Cybersecurity by Using Research, Education, Information, and Technology Act of 2012*, H.R. 4263, 112th Cong., 2nd sess. (27 March 2012): H1641; also *Cyber Intelligence Sharing and Protection Act*, H.R. 3523.RFS, 112th Cong., 2nd sess. (7 May 2012): S2920. SECURE IT died in committee in both houses. CISPA was passed by the House (H.Res.631) but did not make it out of the Senate committee. Industry walked away from negotiations with the Congressional sponsors and no discussions resumed in 2012 after the summer break.

will verify and audit the infrastructure. Furthermore, industry will need to know the appeals process if they disagree with a directed standard; the timeline for confirmed implementation; the penalties for failure; and the list goes on. It is not enough for Congress to say, "Make it so!" without providing detail on its expectations. A full analysis of the specifics and implications of securing U.S. critical infrastructure would be a fine subject for another thesis.

Cyber defense and security of the critical infrastructure is the responsibility of the Department of Homeland Security (DHS). This is a very large mission that the DHS is not yet adequately staffed to execute. There exists a current debate regarding the use of DOD capabilities and expertise as part of the DHS mission to defend the nation, especially given the existence of a military USCYBERCOM and its tasking to operate and defend USG networks, many of which run alongside or overlap with U.S. commercial Internet infrastructure. The DOD and DHS have reached an initial agreement on how DOD technology and expertise might be applied to the DHS mission under a DHS lead, thus avoiding concerns of *posse comitatus* violations.[21] There is much work ahead for the DOD on defense of USG networks and the tentative relationship with DHS for defense of U.S. critical infrastructures. These include a number of interesting and complicated legal and procedural issues worthy of future research and analysis.

As with the laws on cyber crime and cyber security, laws on cyber warfare are similarly nascent. The international community is starting to look at offensive cyber activities in the same way as they address munitions. The International Committee of the

---

[21] U.S. Department of Defense and U.S. Department of Homeland Security, *Memorandum of Agreement between the Department of Homeland Security and the Department of Defense Regarding Cybersecurity* (Washington, DC: Department of Defense and Department of Homeland Security, 2010). *Posse Comitatus* refers to legal limitations placed on the U.S. Armed Forces to limit or deny operations within the borders of the United States.

9

Red Cross has been debating the classification of cyber weapons, not as a type of tool but by the effect that tool might have on a population, and the use of cyber weapons against military versus civilian targets. Nothing has yet been codified in international law, but there is a careful and reasoned debate being carried out.[22] Within the United States, some very basic foreign policy statements are being made on the U.S. position in this arena. Department of State (DOS) Legal Adviser Harold Koh, at a recent inter-agency conference on cyberspace law, spoke at length on the applicability of international law to cyberspace and cyber conflict. He affirmed the position of the USG that the principles of international law apply to cyberspace, to include the law of armed conflict. Additionally, cyber activities may constitute a use of force under Article 2(4) of the United Nations Charter in the event of death, injury, or significant destruction;[23] and a state's right of self-defense under Article 51 is applicable for cyber activities that amount to an armed attack or threat thereof.[24] Mr. Koh's discussion included the fact that these USG positions and points were also agreed upon diplomatically via U.S. engagement with the United Nations Group of Governmental Experts that deals with information technology issues.[25] This collection of official positions on questions many have pondered at length regarding the concept of cyber war is a good first step towards a more rigorous debate.

---

[22] International Committee of the Red Cross, "31st International Conference of the Red Cross and Red Crescent: International Humanitarian Law and the Challenges of Contemporary Armed Conflicts; 28 November – 01 December 2011" (Geneva, CH: ICRC, 2011), 36.

[23] U.S. Department of State, *The United Nations Conference on International Organizations. San Francisco, California, April 25 to June 26, 1945: Selected Documents* (Washington, DC: Government Printing Office, 1946). UN Charter, Article 2(4): "All Members shall refrain in their international relations from the threat or use of force against the territorial integrity or political independence of any state, or in any other manner inconsistent with the Purposes of the United Nations."

[24] Ibid. UN Charter, Article 51: "Nothing in the present Charter shall impair the inherent right of individual or collective self-defence if an armed attack occurs against a Member of the United Nations . . ."

[25] Harold Koh, "International Law in Cyberspace," Opinio Juris blog, transcript posted 19 September 2012, http://opiniojuris.org/2012/09/19/harold-koh-on-international-law-in-cyberspace/ (accessed 30 September 2012).

The fact that this is only a first step is an indicator of how much more work the world has yet to do to establish international norms for this field.[26]

Given this lack of universal understanding and agreement on the application of international law to cyberspace warfare, it should come as no surprise that there is a similar disconnect in U.S. domestic laws about offensive activities. The fact that offensive actions could constitute an attack bordering on armed conflict has not been the focus of the domestic debate; within the USG, the legal argument is over command or control of the activity itself. Attempts made to apply existing laws written for other purposes to the larger question of cyberspace have always resulted in gaping holes in interpretation and widespread disagreement in application. While the USG is actively playing a part in the formulation of international law for cyberspace, it needs to do the same for domestic law.

The core of the discussion in this thesis is the insufficiency or outright lack of appropriate U.S. laws and policies regarding the execution of offensive activities in cyberspace by USG military actors in support of USG military missions. In addition, the discussion will address the current misapplication of U.S. laws and policies that have nothing to do with cyberspace by those who may have a hidden agenda or equities in the arena. What follows are précis of the rest of this document, by chapter, to provide a roadmap for the reader.

---

[26] For a sampling of the debate on the Law of Armed Conflict, International Humanitarian Law, and the applicability to cyberspace, see: Walter Gary Sharp, Sr., *Cyberspace and the Use of Force* (Falls Church, VA: Aegis Research Corporation, 1999); Michael Gervais, *Cyber Attacks and the Laws of War* (New Haven, CT: Yale University School of Law, 2011); Thomas C. Wingfield, *The Law of Information Conflict: National Security Law in Cyberspace* (Falls Church, VA: Aegis Research Corporation, 2000); Herbert Lin, "Offensive Cyber Operations and the Use of Force," *Journal of National Security Law & Policy* 4, no. 1 (2010).

Chapter 2 is "The State of the Cyber Union" – definitions and background to assist a reader who might not be comfortably conversant in this field. It includes a run-down of the major USG actors in the arena, where their respective interests lie, and where there are areas of contention. Further, Chapter 2 delves into why cyberspace is not well understood in the warfighting community – the sophistication of the domain and other key issues. Chapter 2 also addresses the current state of affairs within the USG battle for primacy over offensive actions in cyberspace. To avoid the possibility of accidentally touching upon classified topics, a hypothetical scenario is used to demonstrate the complexity of the standing argument.

Chapter 3 is "What is the Question All About?" – a breakdown of the single most commonly asked question about special or unconventional operations: "Is this Title 10 or Title 50?" The chapter examines what the question means, how it arose, and why the question itself adds to the confusion. The question, as used to look at special operations versus covert paramilitary actions, is starting to be applied to cyberspace by those trying to find a notionally quick answer for a problematic scenario. Chapter 3 includes legislative history over several decades to help the reader understand how the USG arrived at the current state of affairs.

Chapter 4 is "The Cyber Square Peg" – how the different factions behind the debate are trying to force the square peg into a round hole of their particular preference, and why the cyber peg cannot fit into any of these biased holes. The discussion focuses on the misapplication of laws designed for the control and oversight of a completely different mission set, why this misapplication cannot lead to a solution, and additional factors being ignored by both sides of the debate that are of major impact to any way forward for the USG.

Chapter 5 is "Recommendations For A New Hole" – recommendations for a course of action that could put an end to the debate and allow U.S. military commanders to call once again for supporting actions in cyberspace. This process will include clarifying the debate by the application of straightforward guidance and direction on the part of the administration, corresponding legislation by Congress to update the U.S. Code specifically for cyberspace, and the follow-on rollout of information to the DOD warfighting community and the rest of the USG.

CHAPTER 2: THE STATE OF THE CYBER UNION

Military Activities in Cyberspace

Information Operations (IO) has existed as a category of military capabilities for

many years. By Department of Defense (DOD) definition, IO is:

> The integrated employment, during military operations, of information-
> related capabilities in concert with other lines of operation to influence,
> disrupt, corrupt, or usurp the decision-making of adversaries and potential
> adversaries while protecting our own.[1]

IO is a loosely grouped catchall for a number of non-kinetic capabilities used as

supporting functions for conventional kinetic warfare. According to DOD doctrine,

cyberspace operations, traditionally known as Computer Network Operations (CNO), is

one of these supporting functions.[2] CNO is made up of computer network attack (CNA),

computer network defense (CND), and computer network exploitation (CNE).[3] These

traditional terms and their definitions are being updated and joined by emergent

terminology as the DOD's cyberspace community matures in its understanding of the

domain and the implications of operating within it. Additionally, the DOD determined

that the operations of its command and control networks were an inherent part of

defending them and added network operations (NetOps) as an adjunct or associated

function to CND: "activities conducted to operate and defend the Global Information

Grid."[4]

---

[1] U.S. Joint Chiefs of Staff, *Department of Defense Dictionary of Military and Associated Terms*, Joint Publication 1-02 (Washington, DC: Joint Chiefs of Staff, 2010), s.v. "information operations."

[2] U.S. Joint Chiefs of Staff, *Information Operations*, Joint Publication 3-13 (Washington, DC: Joint Chiefs of Staff, 2012), II-9. IO capabilities include Operational Security (OPSEC), Electronic Warfare (EW), Military Information Support Operations (MISO), and Military Deception (MILDEC).

[3] U.S. Joint Chiefs of Staff, *Department of Defense Dictionary*, s.v. "computer network operations."

[4] Ibid., s.v. "computer network defense."

In late 2010, the Vice Chairman of the Joint Chiefs of Staff disseminated a Joint Staff developed "Cyberspace Operations Lexicon" – a first attempt at creating and/or updating common vocabulary for cyberspace lightly aligned with standard joint military terminology. In this lexicon, cyberspace operations (CO) is informally and unsatisfactorily defined as "the employment of cyber capabilities where the primary purpose is to achieve objectives in or through cyberspace,"[5] where cyberspace itself is a "domain characterized by the use of electronics and the electromagnetic spectrum to store, modify, and exchange data via networked systems and associated physical infrastructures."[6] In this same tentative lexicon, offensive cyberspace operations (OCO) include activities to attack, "gather information" (aka CNE), prepare the environment, and actively defend, among others.[7]

With these two different sets of definitions, one doctrinally accepted but now largely outdated, the other overly non-specific and inadequate, it would be easy to confuse the reader. For this discussion, "offensive" as applied to a cyber action will be used in the context of two aggressor-like definitions. First, as cyber attack, "a hostile act . . . to disrupt and/or destroy an adversary's critical cyber systems, assets, or functions,"[8] and as CNA, "actions taken through the use of computer networks to disrupt, deny, degrade, or destroy information resident in computers and computer networks, or the computers and networks themselves."[9] Throughout this thesis, the term "offensive cyberspace activities" (OCA) will be used to avoid disagreements between doctrinal

---

[5] U.S. Joint Chiefs of Staff, *Cyberspace Operations Lexicon* (Washington, DC: Joint Chiefs of Staff, 2010), s.v. "cyberspace operations."
   [6] Ibid., s.v. "cyberspace."
   [7] Ibid., s.v. "offensive cyberspace operations."
   [8] Ibid., s.v. "cyber attack."
   [9] U.S. Joint Chiefs of Staff, *Department of Defense Dictionary*, s.v. "computer network attack."

CNA or the Joint Staff suggested OCO, except when discussing history which predates the Joint Staff lexicon. Finally, specific issues and sensitivities about CNE and operational preparation of the environment as offensive acts in cyberspace will be addressed at appropriate times later in this document.

The Joint Staff lexicon, which was not coordinated across the entire DOD, was a first step towards initiating the effort to write joint doctrine for this rapidly expanding field. Cyberspace operations had become the purview of an entire sub-unified combatant command, U.S. Cyber Command (USCYBERCOM); it naturally followed that CNO doctrine should no longer be a mere function under IO, but a separate doctrinal topic. Joint Publication (JP) 3-12, *Cyberspace Operations*, has existed as a classified draft document since that time, due in part to repeated unsuccessful efforts across the entire DOD to agree upon operational terminology. Broader U.S. policy considerations on the execution of cyberspace operations are other hurdles in finalizing this new joint publication – more on this topic in later chapters. In contrast, the corresponding rewrite to JP 3-13, *Information Operations*, was published in November 2012.[10] Until such time as JP 3-12 is published, the closest thing the DOD has for joint doctrinal guidance for cyberspace are limited portions of the outdated 2006 version of JP 3-13.

Military Actors in Cyberspace

CNO in DOD doctrine is an amalgam of multiple functions, with those functions managed by different organizations. In 1998, DOD created the Joint Task Force CND (JTF-CND) under U.S. Space Command (USSPACECOM). JTF-CND became JTF-CNO in 2000 with the addition of the CNA mission for DOD. In 2002, USSPACECOM

---

[10] U.S. Joint Chiefs of Staff, *Information Operations*.

merged with U.S. Strategic Command (USSTRATCOM) and JTF-CNO aligned as a

component command to conform to the Unified Command Plan (UCP), which placed IO

in USSTRATCOM's mission set.

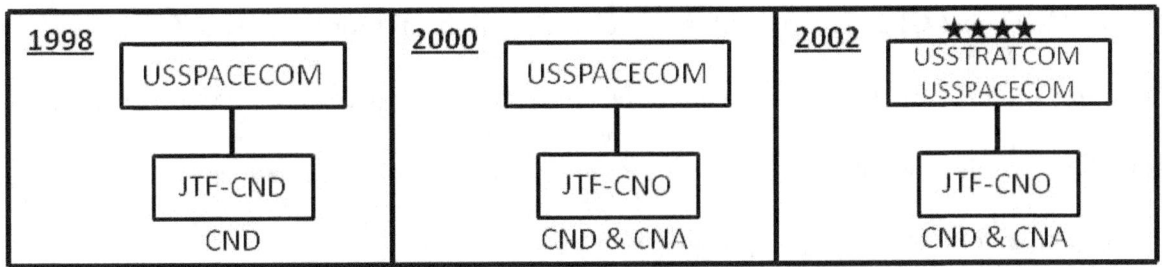

In 2004, the Secretary of Defense (SECDEF) delegated command authority of

JTF-CNO to Director, Defense Information Systems Agency (DISA) to synchronize with

USSTRATCOM's Global Information Grid (GIG) initiative, and renamed the command

JTF-GNO for Global Network Operations, functionally aligning NetOps to CND by

"dual-hatting" – assigning the leadership of both missions to one person.[11] The CNA

mission transferred to an interim organization, which evolved into the Joint Functional

Component Command–Network Warfare (JFCC-NW) in 2005 to be the new DOD lead

for CNA. JFCC-NW was a component under USSTRATCOM, and command authority

for JFCC-NW was dual-hatted to the officer serving as Director, National Security

Agency (DIRNSA); more on this relationship later.

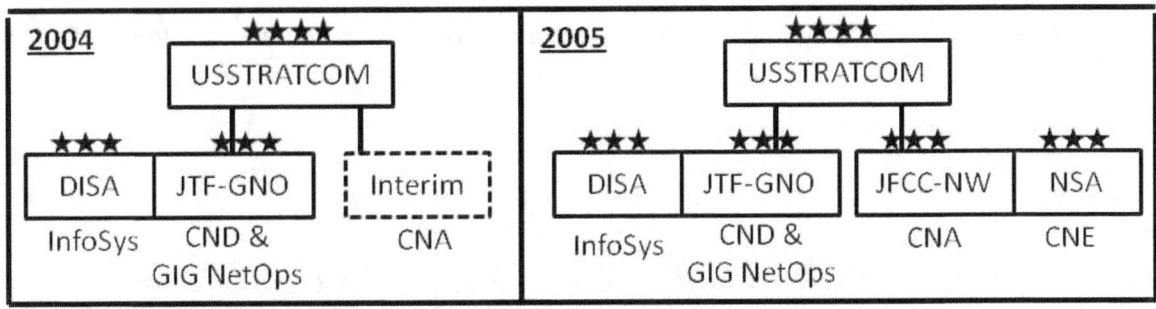

---

[11] *Encarta World English Dictionary*, North American ed., s.v. "dual-hatted." Especially in the
military, a person filling multiple positions or holding multiple authorities is said to be wearing two hats.

In 2009, then SECDEF Robert Gates issued the directive to establish USCYBERCOM as a sub-unified command under USSTRATCOM.[12] To achieve this new Command construct, JFCC-NW first absorbed JTF-GNO, thereby placing all DOD CNA, CND, and GIG NetOps within one chain of command for the first time. JFCC-NW became USCYBERCOM in 2010 upon the confirmation of then LTG Keith Alexander, DIRNSA, to the additional and elevated four-star position of Commander, USCYBERCOM.[13]

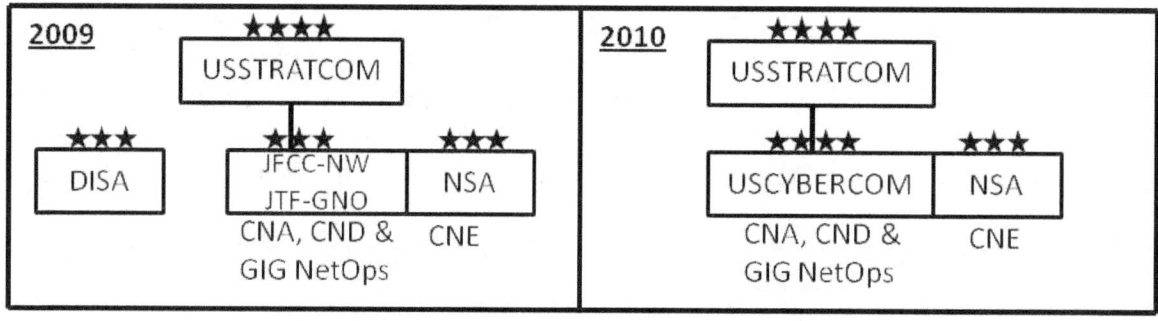

The current mission statement of USCYBERCOM reads as follows:

> USCYBERCOM plans, coordinates, integrates, synchronizes, and conducts activities to: direct the operations and defense of specified Department of Defense information networks and; prepare to, and when directed, conduct full-spectrum military cyberspace operations in order to enable actions in all domains, ensure US/Allied freedom of action in cyberspace and deny the same to our adversaries.[14]

This mission is very broad and particularly complex. The CND and NetOps portions alone are a massive undertaking: according to GEN Alexander, there are roughly 15,000

---

[12] U.S. Secretary of Defense, *Establishment of a Subordinate Unified U.S. Cyber Command Under U.S. Strategic Command for Military Cyberspace Operations* (Washington, DC: Department of Defense, 2009).

[13] U.S. Strategic Command, "United States Strategic Command," http://www.stratcom.mil/ (accessed 21 December 2012).

[14] U.S. Cyber Command, "United States Cyber Command," http://www.cybercom.mil/default.aspx (accessed 21 December 2012).

GIG enclaves and subnets in operation around the world.[15] Realigning the forces and the

funding structures under USCYBERCOM will take a great deal of effort with no small

amount of breakage along the way; however, protecting the DOD's command and control

networks is the primary mission of USCYBERCOM, so enduring the pain is necessary.

This mission set becomes even more complicated where the DOD's GIG exchanges data

with the public and commercial portions of the Internet, both physically and virtually. As

previously mentioned, the DOD defends the homeland beyond U.S. territorial boundaries,

but it is the responsibility of the Department of Homeland Security (DHS) to execute this

mission within U.S. borders. Negotiations continue for effective information sharing

between DOD and DHS.[16]

The OCA mission set is another story. Cyberspace brings with it the

misconception that warfare can be bloodless, which makes it attractive to those who

understand that engaging in a kinetic war is the least desirable thing a nation-state can or

should do. Cyber warfare is appealing to those who desire a quick victory without the

expenditure of physical resources (ordnance, personnel, etc.). In reality, the domain is

not there yet.

Fictional works of literature and theater give the general population a perspective

on cyberspace operations that is well outside the bounds of reality. This false "art of the

possible" often places those knowledgeable persons within the cyber community into the

unenviable position of explaining to leaders and colleagues that just because Jack Bauer

---

[15] Ellen Nakashima, "New Cyber Command Chief Warns of Possible Attacks; U.S. Military Networks in War Zones could be Targeted, Alexander Says," *Washington Post*, 04 June 2010; Keith B. Alexander, "Mission Success in Cyberspace," *Military Information Technology,* July 2010.

[16] U.S. Department of Defense and U.S. Department of Homeland Security, *Memorandum of Agreement between the Department of Homeland Security and the Department of Defense regarding Cybersecurity* (Washington, DC: Department of Defense and Department of Homeland Security, 2010).

did something on *24*[17] it does not mean that the U.S. government (USG) actually has either the capability or the legal authorities to replicate that action. More often than not, the legal questions are the most often misunderstood facet of an operation and the major limiting factor for executing an offensive action in cyberspace, more so even than whether or not a technical solution exists to carry out the action.

Cyberspace is an ever-evolving technological challenge. Keeping up with the changes in security capabilities and network implementation standards across a worldwide infrastructure is nearly impossible given that there is no single organization directing Internet configurations or access and usage policies beyond basic network addressing protocols and domain names.[18] It is left to the various network service providers around the world to implement their particular portions of the Internet to the minimum routing and addressing standards, with anything above or beyond that minimum being solely at their discretion based upon their business model, their client set, and their own assessments of the environment. In order to operate effectively in the cyberspace domain, the DOD must apply a massive level of continuous investment in personnel, research, expertise, and equipment just to maintain status quo.

Specific details of both offensive and defensive USG cyberspace capabilities are closely held secrets for very good reasons. Keeping sensitive details within a restricted need-to-know community is good operational security for any endeavor. It is just as important for a defender to protect the details of his defense mechanisms as it is for an attacker to protect his assault plan, especially for cyberspace.

---

[17] *24*, FOX – Fox Broadcasting Company, 2001-2010.
[18] ICANN – Internet Corporation for Assigned Names and Numbers. Responsible for Internet Protocol (IP) address management and the registration of top-level domain names (.com, .org, .net, etc.).

In addition to the sensitivity of the information itself, the complexity of cyberspace and the level of technical knowledge required to understand the implications of an action or the limitations of it is beyond the comprehension level of most laypersons. Computers, communications systems, and the rest of telecommunications infrastructures are even more complex. Cyberspace is an area of operation where one cannot merely get by with a basic knowledge of the domain, and attempts to simplify the details often trivialize the complexity and may lead to further misunderstanding based on a false perception of knowledge.

The complexity of cyberspace is the most significant reason behind the creation of a single center for OCA within the DOD. By requiring centralized coordination and planning for a particular set of operations, the DOD ensures consistent application of the policies, laws, and current technology by those who are well versed in the subject. This centralized coordination brings some economy of scale to the application of cyberspace expertise to the customer community, and decreases the time necessary to develop subject-matter experts. By existing in an immersion environment, personnel learn at a faster rate and with a greater depth of understanding of the potential impact of cyber actions, both the successes and failures. The corresponding application of this expertise across the spectrum of customers may be better synchronized and prioritized when there is one central clearinghouse for requirements. Tools may be developed outside of the hub, but the rules and guidance that determine when and how a tool may be used are more consistent when written by a central source. For example, Smith & Wesson and Glock both make pistols, but not the rules governing the use of deadly force.[19] Finally,

---

[19] For public domain discussion of the development of cyber weapons, see: Ellen Nakashima, "Defense Dept. Develops List of Cyber-Weapons," *Washington Post*, 01 June 2011; Ellen Nakashima,

the ability to apply the capabilities of a particular tool to a given situation in order to achieve a desired effect is a level of operational art that only comes to users (i.e. cyber planners) with time and experience.

Beyond the DOD, there are other USG entities with interests in operating in or through cyberspace. The Federal Bureau of Investigation (FBI), part of the Department of Justice (DOJ), is tasked with policing U.S. cyberspace from a law enforcement perspective. They pursue individuals engaged in cyber crime (intrusions, denial of service) or who use cyberspace as a tool to support other criminal activity (theft, child pornography, etc.).[20] The intelligence community (IC) uses cyberspace to further the mission sets of its respective members; due to classification restrictions, discussions on missions or capabilities of the IC in cyberspace will necessarily be limited in this document. To aid the deconfliction of the full spectrum of operations in cyberspace carried out by these disparate departments and agencies of the USG, a three-way agreement exists between the DOD, DOJ, and IC as to how they coordinate operations in cyberspace to avoid possible interference between signatories.[21] This attempt at coordination has not been completely successful; a significant breakdown in deconfliction will be discussed at length later in this chapter.

OCA is a relatively new field of operations for the DOD and the rest of the USG; as such, the resources necessary for the execution of these activities are not yet in place. Although USCYBERCOM exists, it is not a fully functioning self-contained

---

"Cyberweapons on Pentagon Fast Track," *Washington Post*, 10 April 2012; Ellen Nakashima, "U.S. Accelerating Cyberweapon Reseach," *Washington Post*, 18 March 2012.

[20] Federal Bureau of Investigation, "What we Investigate - Cyber Crime," http://www.fbi.gov/about-us/investigate/cyber (accessed 21 December 2012).

[21] U.S. Department of Defense, U.S. Department of Justice, and Intelligence Community, <*Title Omitted*> (Washington, DC: Department of Defense, Department of Justice, and Intelligence Community, 2007). This three-way agreement between the DOD, DOJ, and IC is a classified document, the title of which is (U//FOUO), so it cannot be cited explicitly in this document.

organization. USCYBERCOM does not yet have its own budget to execute (operational funds come from USSTRATCOM, support from NSA), direction of manpower requirements, nor a headquarters building (it is currently housed within NSA facilities on Fort George G. Meade, MD).[22] In addition, the DOD cyber community is faced with a military customer set with a limited understanding of what cyberspace is, let alone how supporting operations in cyberspace might aid in a larger campaign. The operations community lacks sufficient personnel who understand the breadth and depth of OCA effects in order to bring them to bear in support of a joint force commander. There is not yet an educational pipeline for the military services to train and provide cyberspace personnel to any accepted standard, nor the ability to retain personnel with highly marketable skills in the commercial sector.[23] Finally, the DOD and others within the USG do not agree as to the policies and laws governing the use of offensive capabilities in cyberspace, leading to the current battle for primacy in cyberspace.

The Cease Fire

As previously discussed, JFCC-NW was assigned as the lead for all DOD offensive cyberspace activities in 2005; in contrast, no lead designation was specified for non-DOD actions. Through the latter years of JFCC-NW, there existed an unchartered panel of inter-agency points of contact engaged in regular discussions and updates on the

---

[22] U.S. Cyber Command, "United States Cyber Command," http://www.cybercom.mil/default.aspx (accessed 21 December 2012).

[23] Ellen Nakashima and Brian Krebs, "As Cyberattacks Increase, U.S. Faces Shortage of Security Talent," *Washington Post*, 23 December 2009; "U.S. Short on Offensive-Mission Cyber Experts," *Federal Times*, 09 July 2012. See also House Armed Services Committee, "U.S. Cyber Command: Organizing for Cyberspace Operations," 111th Cong, 2nd sess., 2010. In his testimony, GEN Alexander, Commander, USCYBERCOM and Director, NSA said, "The biggest challenge we currently face is generating the people we need to do this mission. I am optimistic we will get the force we need. We are pushing on the Services to go faster to bring those forces in. My greatest concern is moving fast enough to provide a capability to defend our networks in time were a crisis to occur. We see that as our No. 1 mission - be ready."

state of affairs for their respective cyberspace operational planning and execution.[24] This

panel provided an unofficial forum for operational deconfliction at the action officer

level. If agreement could not be reached via this panel, the operation would come under

the purview of the previously mentioned DOD-DOJ-IC agreement for resolution. One

limitation of both the panel and the three-way agreement was the lack of a veto authority

amongst the signatories – a simple majority could allow an activity to proceed against the

concerns of a dissenting position.

In the 2008-2009 timeframe, JFCC-NW allegedly engaged in one or more

cyberspace operations that conflicted with one or more CIA operations in the Middle

East, allegedly angering one or more foreign partners of the CIA, including Saudi

Arabia.[25] In response to this operation and the perceived disregard for deconfliction with

on-going intelligence operations, the CIA officially requested a review of U.S. law

associated with cyberspace operations.[26] The CIA made the assertion that offensive

cyberspace activities fall under the definition of covert actions, and therefore were not to

be undertaken by any organization of the USG except for the CIA, and only under very

specific circumstances.[27] There has been no official resolution to this question: U.S. law

is very non-specific or even non-existent on the subject of cyberspace operations, so any

ruling or interpretation could be seen as an attempt at creating a precedent where no legal

basis exists. Until a ruling on the covert action question is released, all offensive cyber

---

[24] Ellen Nakashima, "For Cyberwarriors, Murky Terrain; Pentagon's Dismantling of Saudi-CIA Web Site Illustrates Need for Clearer Policies," *Washington Post*, 19 March 2010.
[25] Ibid.
[26] Ellen Nakashima, "Pentagon is Debating Cyber-Attacks," *Washington Post*, 06 November 2010.
[27] 50 USC § 401: E.O. 12333 1.7(a)(4).

operations by the U.S. military that would occur outside a "theater of war"[28] are

effectively on an operational stand-down. [29] A discussion of covert action is covered in

Chapter 3. The question of whether covert action applies to cyberspace is discussed in

Chapter 4. Recommendations for a way out of this state of limbo will be the outcome of

this thesis, addressed in Chapter 5. To aid in understanding the impact of the theater of

war question on U.S. military cyberspace operations, what follows is a hypothetical

scenario with fictional actors to exemplify some of the issues at work and the language in

use.

Elbonia is a nation-state somewhere in the middle of Eastern Europe, largely

covered in waist-deep mud.[30] Elbonia has neighboring nations with which it enjoys good

relations, Anklia and Wristland. In contrast, Kneebonia, Elbonia's neighbor to the south,

has been a continuing source of discord in the region, engaging in random acts of

unfriendly behavior for decades. The most recent of these unfriendly acts was to lob

repeated volleys of garbage in the general vicinity of Elbonia's capital city. The

Elbonian government decides to put an end to this trash barrage, and comes up with a

plan: the military will execute an aerial carpet-mudding campaign on the Kneebonian

launch facility. To do this, they must neutralize the Kneebonian anti-air defenses in

advance of the sortie. Through their spy network, the Elbonians know that the

Kneebonians use an old Commodore-64 computer to run their defense system. The

Elbonians also know that the Kneebonians have no one smart enough to operate their

---

[28] U.S. Joint Chiefs of Staff, *Department of Defense Dictionary*, s.v. "theater of war." ". . . the area of air, land, and water that is, or may become, directly involved in the conduct of major operations and campaigns involving combat."
    [29] Nakashima, "Pentagon is Debating Cyber-Attacks."
    [30] Profuse apologies and thanks to Scott Adams, creator of the *Dilbert©* comic strip wherein we encounter the Elbonians and Kneebonians as inhabitants of fictional fourth-world nations at odds with each other; (Distributed by Universal Uclick, Kansas City, MO).

networks, so they hire technical support from neighboring Wristland. They have placed their Commodore-64 in a Wristland-based computer facility for ease of access by the network administrators. In this configuration, for Elbonia to execute a cyber attack on the Kneebonian anti-air system, they would have to conduct offensive acts against a network infrastructure existing within a friendly third country, namely Wristland. This action would occur outside of the theater of war (i.e., outside of Kneebonia), even though the effects of the cyber action would be felt inside Kneebonia. Of additional concern is whether the Wristlandese might be negatively affected if the Elbonian attack were to go awry and somehow damage the Wristland network infrastructure. Should Elbonia warn its Ambassador to Wristland of the impending attack, in the event that something does go wrong and the Wristland network administrators start asking uncomfortable questions? To make matters more politically complex, the Elbonian Ministry of Foreign Relations objects to both the aerial campaign and the supporting cyber attack because of the potential for creating additional unfriendly feelings in both Kneebonia and Wristland.

In this not-as-farcical-as-it-may-seem scenario, Kneebonia is the theater of war, giving the Elbonian military commander primacy for operational planning and execution within those boundaries. The difficulty exists when achieving a desired effect within the theater would require action external to the theater. Under the current U.S. restrictions, the Elbonian military would be barred from executing the supporting cyber operation against the Kneebonian Commodore-64 located in Wristland. As a result, the Elbonian pilot would have to attempt his flight in spite of the anti-air barrage, decreasing the likelihood of success of his mission. As an aside, U.S. regulations for targeting a person, place, or thing for both kinetic and non-kinetic action require confirmed knowledge of the location of the target for a legal authorities review.

In the case where active warfare has not yet begun, the definition of a theater of war becomes extremely problematic. The use of cyberspace operations to aid in setting or shaping the theater for an operational campaign continues to run into non-military objections regarding the determination of operational necessity.[31] Propaganda campaigns and the countering thereof are prime scenarios. For example, a not-yet-hostile nation posts propaganda to a webpage somewhere in the world that offends U.S. sensibilities in some way. Given the fact that a state of war does not yet exist, could the U.S. military justify cyber action to remove or alter the propaganda? Regardless of the end-state, the offensive cyberspace action would be targeting infrastructure outside of a theater of war.[32] Finally, any action taken would expose access and capabilities to the potential adversary, thereby running the risk that they would take appropriate defensive measures to block further cyberspace operations, negating the use of the capability at some time in the future.[33]

This situation and the series of seemingly unanswerable hypothetical questions actually exists today in the USG, stifling the development of meaningful rules of engagement for cyberspace, proper implementation and integration procedures for cyber operations with conventional military activities, and a useful level of expertise within the practitioners necessary to advance the field. Chapter 3 will go into detail on the CIA's

---

[31] U.S. Joint Chiefs of Staff, *Department of Defense Dictionary*, s.v. "operational necessity." "A mission associated with war or peacetime operations in which the consequences of an action justify the risk of loss . . ."

[32] Nakashima, "For Cyberwarriors, Murky Terrain."

[33] Ellen Nakashima, "Pentagon Officials had Weighed Cyberattack on Gaddafi's Air Defenses," *Washington Post*, 18 October 2011.

claim of covert action and will provide a plain-language discussion of the U.S. laws whereby historical precedence and legislative wrangling have left room for someone to register a procedural complaint, bringing the Title 10 offensive cyberspace community to a virtual standstill.

CHAPTER 3: WHAT IS THE QUESTION ALL ABOUT?

In early May of 2011, Leon Panetta, then Director of the Central Intelligence

Agency (CIA), described the Abbottabad operation as follows:

> Since this was what is called a "Title 50" operation, which is a covert
> operation, and it comes directly from the President of the United States
> who made the decision to conduct this operation in a covert way, that
> direction goes to me. And then, I am, you know, the person who then
> commands the mission. But having said that, I have to tell you that the
> real commander was Admiral McRaven because he was on site, and he
> was actually in charge of the military operation that went in and got bin
> Laden.[1]

Mr. Panetta is a lawyer, with additional background in Congress, appropriations, and

public policy issues.[2] He was deeply involved in the planning and execution of this

activity and had a significant number of lawyers who specialize in U.S. military and

intelligence law upon whom to call. If Mr. Panetta could casually misuse terminology in

such a way as to inadvertently misrepresent the U.S. laws and authorities at work for this

mission, it is not at all surprising that the general operations community has trouble

comprehending the complexity. As a result, the operations community finds itself faced

with the often-asked question, "Is this a Title 10 or Title 50 op?" by persons not

sufficiently educated in the details to understand the answer and its implications. The

following sections will simplify the language and the application of U.S. law and provide

a brief history on the question to provide a backdrop for the rest of this thesis.

Title 10 versus Title 50 – the Basics

What is the question? What does "is this Title 10 or Title 50?" really mean? Title

---

[1] Leon Panetta, interview by Jim Lehrer, *PBS Newshour*, 03 May 2011, PBS,
http://www.pbs.org/newshour/bb/terrorism/jan-june11/panetta_05-03.html (accessed 14 December 2012.
[2] U.S. Department of Defense, "Biography of Leon E Panetta, Secretary of Defense,"
http://www.defense.gov/bios/biographydetail.aspx?biographyid=310 (accessed 14 December 2012).

10 of the U.S. Code is "Armed Forces." It outlines and documents the basis in U.S. law for the roles, missions, and organization of the U.S. Department of Defense (DOD) to include the uniformed services of the DOD: Army, Navy, Marine Corps, Air Force, and the reserve components of each. For example, Title 10 includes the Uniform Code of Military Justice (UCMJ),[3] military law enacted by Congress for "…the Government and Regulation of the land and naval forces."[4] Title 10 gives the Secretary of Defense (SECDEF) all "authority, direction and control" over the DOD.[5] Title 10 further describes how the DOD documents and reports on all activities executed under the authorities of the SECDEF. Most Title 10 operations and activities are carried out by armed forces personnel under a direct command structure leading up through the SECDEF to the President in his role as Commander-in-Chief.[6] When used as shorthand, "Title 10" is usually meant to indicate a military activity under military command and authorities.

Title 50 of the U.S. Code is "War and National Defense." It is a large catchall of items pertaining to warfare (weaponry, spoils of war, counter-proliferation, etc.), U.S. intelligence activities, espionage against the United States, and a host of other topics unrelated to this discussion. For the purposes of this thesis, the most significant facet of Title 50 is that it defines and outlines the notification and reporting requirements of the application of intelligence authorities by the elements of the Intelligence Community (IC). It includes confirmation that the SECDEF executes administrative control over those members of the IC who are DOD entities (for example, DIA – Defense Intelligence

---

[3] 10 USC§ 801 et seq.
[4] U.S. Constitution, Article 1, Section 8.
[5] 10 USC § 113(b).
[6] U.S. Constitution, Article 2.

Agency, and NSA – National Security Agency).[7] Title 50 operations by IC member elements are carried out under an intelligence line of authority via the Director of National Intelligence (DNI) to the President as Chief Executive.[8] When used as shorthand, "Title 50" is usually meant to indicate an intelligence activity under non-military control and authorities headed by one of the three-letter Agencies within the IC, most often the CIA or the NSA.

The fact that shorthand exists is because there is a perceived need to simplify the discussion. The problem with this particular shorthand is that it is often interpreted to be an either-or determinant – an easy way of pigeonholing various types of personnel, activities, operations, and authorities for simplified comprehension and processing. Unfortunately, this shorthand is far too broad and often misleading, as will be explained.

Complications arise from the use of the shorthand due to a number of reasons, primarily the fact that it is neither the type of activity itself nor the type of personnel involved that determines the pigeonhole; rather it is the source of the tasking and authority for executing the activity that defines the hole. DOD operations under Title 10 and CIA actions under Title 50 often "may be indistinguishable to the naked eye . . . get kind of merged,"[9] due to a similarity between some of the activities, especially those by U.S. military special operations forces (SOF) and CIA paramilitary personnel. This

---

[7] 50 USC § 401. The Intelligence Community is composed of these elements: the Central Intelligence Agency; the Defense Intelligence Agency; the National Security Agency; the National Reconnaissance Office; the National Geospatial-Intelligence Agency; the intelligence and counter-intelligence elements of the Army, Navy, Air Force, and Marine Corps; intelligence elements of the Federal Bureau of Investigation; intelligence and counter-intelligence elements of the Coast Guard; the Bureau of Intelligence and Research, Department of State; the Office of Intelligence and Analysis, Department of the Treasury; the Office of National Security Intelligence, Drug Enforcement Administration; the Office of Intelligence and Analysis, Department of Homeland Security; and the Office of Intelligence and Counterintelligence, Department of Energy.

[8] 50 USC § 401: E.O. 12333.

[9] Senate Select Committee on Intelligence, Nomination of General Michael V. Hayden, USAF to be Director of the Central Intelligence Agency, 109th Cong., 2nd sess., 2006.

"indistinguishable" view of activities will be discussed in detail later in this chapter. The subject is further muddled in the case of inter-agency operations. For example, CIA personnel assigned to support a military (Title 10) operation would still be themselves operating under the CIA's Title 50 authorities in the provision of that support; likewise, a military unit may provide support to a CIA (Title 50) activity while maintaining their Title 10 operating authorization. The authorities governing the operation or activity must be viewed separately from the authorities controlling the personnel involved in the operation. In other words, a "Title 50 operation" or "Title 10 operation" are so named because of the statutory basis for the mission control authorities only. Mission authority does not preclude the use of personnel or equipment from other U.S. Government (USG) agencies or departments in support of the mission so long as the statutory authorities of the other agency or department permit said support. These authorities are not mutually exclusive and may be mutually beneficial if exercised appropriately, as described in both of the support scenarios just described.

Finally, under Title 50 there exists a sub-category of intelligence activities[10] called covert action.[11] By statute, covert action is defined as:

> . . .an activity or activities of the United States Government to influence political, economic, or military conditions abroad, where it is intended that the role of the United States Government will not be apparent or acknowledged publicly.[12]

Executive Order (E.O.) 12333 directs the CIA to:

> . . . conduct covert action activities approved by the President. No agency except the Central Intelligence Agency . . . may conduct any covert action

---

[10] There is no statutory definition of "intelligence activities." E.O. 12333 broadly discusses intelligence activities as "all activities that elements of the Intelligence Community are authorized to conduct pursuant to this order," a self-referencing circular definition at best.
[11] 50 USC § 413(f).
[12] 50 USC § 413b(e).

activity unless the President determines that another agency is more likely to achieve a particular objective.[13]

These two clauses of Title 50 add a significant complication to the mix, most especially because the definition is very broad and the directive is very specific, leaving room for wordsmiths to obfuscate any legal wrangling amongst USG entities engaged in a debate about operational authorities. Not all CIA activities are covert actions, nor are all other intelligence activities covert actions. Military forces may carry out intelligence activities. Executing any activity (intelligence or military) anonymously and secretively does not necessarily make it a covert action. Therefore, the question should be "is it a Title 10 military operation, a Title 50 intelligence activity, or a Title 50 covert action?"

Intelligence Oversight

To understand today's legal quandary, one must understand the process whereby the USC evolved into its current language.[14] In the post-Vietnam War era, Congress put limitations on the CIA following investigations into a significant number of unreported covert military activities across Southeast Asia. The Hughes-Ryan Amendment to the Foreign Assistance Act of 1974 required that the President report "in a timely fashion" all covert operations of the CIA to "the appropriate" Congressional committees if U.S. funds were to be expended in foreign support actions.[15] While the community commonly used the term "covert action", it had yet to be defined in statute, leaving room for

---

[13] 50 USC § 401: E.O. 12333 1.7(a)(4).

[14] This section draws heavily from several reports of the Congressional Research Service (CRS): *Sensitive Covert Action Notifications: Oversight Options for Congress,* R40691 (Washington, DC: CRS, 2012); *Covert Action: Legislative Background and Possible Policy Questions,* RL33715 (Washington, DC: CRS, 2011); *"Gang of Four" Congressional Intelligence Notifications,* R40698 (Washington, DC: CRS, 2012); *U.S. Special Operations Forces (SOF): Background and Issues for Congress,* RS21048 (Washington, DC: CRS, 2012); *Special Operations Forces (SOF) and CIA Paramilitary Operations: Issues for Congress,* RS22017 (Washington, DC: CRS, 2009).

[15] Foreign Assistance Act of 1974, Public Law 93-559, *U.S. Statutes at Large* 88 (1974): 1795.

interpretation in application.

Following a series of revelations by then New York Times reporter Seymour Hersh that U.S. intelligence agencies were engaged in spying on U.S. citizens[16] and the corroboratory results from the Church Committee and other congressional investigations, Congress acted to overturn its long-standing unwritten policy of "benign neglect" of intelligence oversight.[17] In 1976 and 1977, respectively, Congress established the Senate Select Committee on Intelligence (SSCI) and the House Permanent Select Committee on Intelligence (HPSCI) to provide oversight of intelligence activities. After the failed rescue attempt in 1980 of the Iran Embassy hostages, Congress responded with the Intelligence Authorization Act for 1981 that repealed the Hughes-Ryan amendment, replacing past soft language on reporting with the mandate that all U.S. departments and agencies specifically keep the two Congressional Intelligence Committees "fully and currently informed of all intelligence activities." For extremely sensitive operations, the President may limit the advance notification to a small subset of Intelligence Committee members. However, if prior notice is withheld, the President is required to inform the committees in an undefined "timely fashion" and provide a statement of the reasons for not giving prior notice.[18]

In the wake of the Iran-Contra affair, then President Ronald Reagan issued a directive prohibiting retroactive findings and requiring that all presidential findings be in

---

[16] Seymour M. Hersh published many articles in this vein from late 1974 onwards, to include: "Huge C.I.A. Operation Reported in U.S. Against Antiwar Forces, Other Dissidents in Nixon Years," *New York Times*, 22 December 1974; "Underground for the C.I.A. in New York: An Ex-Agent Tells of Spying on Students," *New York Times*, 29 December 1974; "C.I.A. Admits Domestic Acts, Denies 'Massive' Illegality," *New York Times*, 16 January 1975.

[17] Loch K. Johnson, "The Church Committee Investigation of 1975 and the Evolution of Modern Intelligence Accountability," *Intelligence and National Security* 23, no.2 (April 2008): 204.

[18] Intelligence Authorization Act for Fiscal Year 1981, Public Law 96-450, *U.S. Statutes at Large* 94 (1980): 1981.

written form.[19] As a legal definition, a finding is a "determination by a judge, jury, or administrative agency of a fact supported by the evidence in the record."[20] In the covert action sphere, a finding is the vehicle documenting Presidential determination that a foreign policy situation exists somewhere in the world requiring action to protect and support U.S. national interests, and directs that such action be taken.[21] Title 50 defaults control over covert actions to the CIA unless otherwise directed by the President.[22]

Using the recommendations of the Congressional Iran-Contra Committee, the SSCI constructed new statutory reporting requirements to tighten up their oversight responsibilities. The first version of this legislation was pocket-vetoed by then President George H.W. Bush due to a lack of consistency between the stated intent of the oversight guidance and the actual text of the law.[23] Congress returned the bill to conference, inserted new language on their intent regarding several points of the legislation, left the details of their intent within the body of the conference proceedings rather than in the text of the bill itself, and the bill was subsequently signed into law by President Bush. Unfortunately, the fact that Congress omitted including descriptive language within the law itself opened the door for future legal challenges to interpretation of the text since conference proceedings and committee notes are not legally binding.

This legislation provided the first statutory definition for covert action, which

---

[19] U.S. President, National Security Decision Directive, "Approval and Review of Special Activities," declassified extract from NSDD-286, http://www.reagan.utexas.edu/archives/reference/Scanned NSDDS/NSDD286.pdf (accessed 14 January 2013).

[20] *Black's Law Dictionary*, 9th ed., s.v. "finding."

[21] 50 USC § 413b(a).

[22] 50 USC § 401: E.O. 12333 1.7(a)(4).

[23] U.S. President, "Memorandum of Disapproval for the Intelligence Authorization Act, Fiscal Year 1991," George Bush Presidential Library and Museum, http://bushlibrary.tamu.edu/research/public_papers.php?id=2520&year=1990&month=11 (accessed 19 January 2013)..

remains in place today. It also elevated responsibility for reporting of all intelligence

activities to the President vice the heads of the departments or agencies executing those

activities.[24] This Presidential responsibility has since been delegated to the DNI, in

concert with the self-same heads of the IC elements.[25]

The final report of the 9/11 Commission included recommendations for Congress

itself.[26] The Commission recognized that Congressional oversight and information

management of intelligence is weakened by the fact that different committees within the

House and Senate control authorizations for activities vice appropriations of funds for

those activities. The annual Intelligence Authorization Act (IAA) is the vehicle by which

the Intelligence Committees approve and direct operations and programs within the

Intelligence Community. The intelligence budget, which includes monies to execute

these authorized operations and programs, is largely included in the annual DOD budget.

As such, defense subcommittees of the congressional appropriations process control the

final IC budget and not the Intelligence Committees themselves. Absent an approved

IAA for a given fiscal year, Congress moves forward with the budget process by

including non-specific catchall language in the defense appropriations to allow

intelligence activities to continue, but this process does not allow for a line-by-line

review of the activities by the Intelligence Committees. The fact that the Intelligence

Committees have failed to enact intelligence authorization bills before budget process

deadlines for much of the past decade further self-limited their oversight of intelligence

---

[24] Intelligence Authorization Act for Fiscal Year 1991, Public Law 102-88, *U.S. Statutes at Large* 105 (1991): 429.

[25] Intelligence Reform and Terrorism Prevention Act of 2004, Public Law 108-458, *U.S. Statutes at Large* 118 (2004): 3644. IRTPA created the position of Director of National Intelligence (DNI).

[26] National Commission on Terrorist Attacks upon the United States, *The 9/11 Commission Report: Final Report of the National Commission on Terrorist Attacks upon the United States* (New York, NY: Norton, 2004), 419-423.

activities. Congress might complain about the issues associated with intelligence oversight, but much of it is self-inflicted pain.

Special Operations Oversight

Contrasting the oversight requirements for special operations forces (SOF) with those of intelligence activities require several definitions up front. The DOD defines special operations as:

> Operations requiring unique modes of employment, tactical techniques, equipment and training often conducted in hostile, denied, or politically sensitive environments and characterized by one or more of the following: time sensitive, clandestine, low visibility, conducted with and/or through indigenous forces, requiring regional expertise, and/or a high degree of risk.[27]

It naturally follows that SOF are "forces of the military . . . specifically organized, trained, and equipped to conduct and support special operations."[28] In comparison, paramilitary forces are "distinct from the regular armed forces . . . but resembling them in organization, equipment, training, or mission."[29] Adding further fog to the arena, DOD defines a covert *operation* as one "that is so planned and executed as to conceal the identity of or permit plausible denial by the sponsor."[30] Finally, a clandestine operation is:

> . . . sponsored or conducted by governmental departments or agencies in such a way as to assure secrecy or concealment. A clandestine operation differs from a covert operation in that emphasis is placed on concealment of the operation rather than on concealment of the identity of the sponsor. In special operations, an activity may be both covert and clandestine. . .[31]

There is no statutory definition of clandestine to compare with that of the DOD.

---

[27] U.S. Joint Chiefs of Staff, *Department of Defense Dictionary of Military and Associated Terms,* Joint Publication 1-02 (Washington, DC: Joint Chiefs of Staff, 2010), s.v. "special operations."
[28] Ibid., s.v. "special operations forces."
[29] Ibid., s.v. "paramilitary forces."
[30] Ibid., s.v. "covert operation."
[31] Ibid., s.v. "clandestine operation."

Congressional oversight of the military is largely straightforward in that it is the joint purview of the House and Senate Armed Services Committees (HASC and SASC, respectively). SOF are Title 10 military forces whose utilization is the responsibility of U.S. Special Operations Command (USSOCOM), a unified combatant command with specific functional command authorities outlined in the *Unified Command Plan* (UCP).[32] Congress created USSOCOM in 1987 to address a perceived need in the DOD for a centralized and common posture for training of SOF and planning of special operations across the services. Since that time, USSOCOM has been designated as the DOD lead organization for all counter-terrorism activities in the Department, making them the DOD prime interlocutor for inter-agency coordination with any other branch of the government for this mission.[33]

Various past examples demonstrate how an observer could be confused between SOF and CIA as an activity progresses.[34] In real time, these sorts of activities might have both groups operating in the area, often working together, with only a little of the detail explained or shared back at headquarters beyond a small circle of those with a need-to-know. Indeed, since December 2004, it has been required by law that DOD and CIA create and use joint procedures to "improve the coordination and deconfliction of operations that involve elements" of the CIA and DOD.[35] Absent first-hand knowledge of this required deconfliction, the indistinguishable nature of the activities on the ground makes the characterization of the operation more difficult by the outside observer,

---

[32] U.S. President, *Unified Command Plan* (Washington, DC: The White House, 2011), 25-27.

[33] Senate Armed Services Committee, *Posture Statement of Admiral William H. McRaven, USN, Commander, United States Special Operations Command*, 112th Cong., 2nd sess., 2012.

[34] Vietnam Theater, early 1960s, CIA supply-chain interdiction in Laos and MAC-V SOG; Nicaragua, 1980s, SOF training Contras who were receiving funds from the CIA; Afghanistan, 2001, CIA paying funds to the warlords of the Northern Alliance while SOF units supplied weapons and ground coordination for air strikes against the Taliban.

[35] Intelligence Reform and Terrorism Prevention Act: 3662-3663.

inducing misinterpretations.

On a related thread, the National Defense Authorization Act for Fiscal Year 2004 included a requirement that the President or the SECDEF must authorize any USSOCOM-led missions.[36] In the fiscal year 2012 National Defense Authorization Act, the SECDEF is required to notify the congressional committees ". . . expeditiously, and in any event in not less than 48 hours, of the use of such authority with respect to that operation." [37] The referenced authority is to expend funds "in support of foreign forces, irregular forces, groups, or individuals supporting or facilitating ongoing military ops by U.S. SOF to combat terrorism."[38] As evidenced here, the language used by those in the Congressional defense establishment has begun to resemble that of those in the intelligence and covert action community, further adding to the perceived convergence of the two statutory lines.

All of this history and the legislative actions to carry out oversight provide another reason why people must ask the "is this Title 10 or Title 50?" question. They ask because the requirements for the preparation, authorization, and post-reporting of the operation will change depending upon the answer. If the answer to the question fails to line up with the execution of the requirements, one risks the public wrath or censure of Congress and a high likelihood of increased oversight.

The Overlap in Oversight

The bulk of day-to-day intelligence and military activities do not conflict with this

---

[36] National Defense Authorization Act for Fiscal Year 2004, Public Law 108-136, *U.S. Statutes at Large* 117 (2003): 1560.

[37] National Defense Authorization Act for Fiscal Year 2009, Public Law 110-417, *U.S. Statutes at Large* 122 (2008): 4356.

[38] National Defense Authorization Act for Fiscal Year 2005, Public Law 108-375, *U.S. Statutes at Large* 118 (2004): 2086.

oversight debate, and are managed quietly and cleanly. It is usually only in the arena of special operations, so-called black ops, "Secret Squirrel,"[39] or anything else that smells of being especially outside of the norm that causes Congress to pay special attention.

Photo Removed Due to Copyright Restrictions

Figure 1: Congressional Oversight of Intelligence Activities and Military Operations[40]

The gray area in the middle of Figure 1 is the cause of disagreement in this realm. Congress itself is responsible for there being a question in the first place: had Congress been more willing to include very clear directive language into the text of legislation in 1990 vice using committee conference reports as interpretation guidance for the community at large, much of the finger-pointing of recent years might have been avoided. Congress has failed to keep pace with the changing world environment in

---

[39] "Secret Squirrel" was a Hanna-Barbera cartoon character of the 1960s who spoofed the traits of James Bond and other well-known fictional spies. The term is used colloquially to denote persons or operations associated with sensitive topics or classified information.

[40] Andru E. Wall, "Demystifying the Title 10-Title 50 Debate: Distinguishing Military Operations, Intelligence Activities & Covert Action," *Harvard National Security Journal* 3, no. 1 (September 2011): 103.

which USG personnel are required to operate. A sizeable body of work exists with analyses of the existing situation and some low impact ways in which the gray area of confusing and obsolete oversight rules might be resolved, but Congress has not yet opted to move towards a solution.[41]

Returning to the definition of covert action, there exists within the language of Title 50 a number of exclusions – rough descriptors of types of activities that are specifically designated as not covert actions.[42] These exclusions were intended to account for other activities that may regularly be conducted secretively and anonymously. This provides the basis for the legal loophole discussion most often used to avoid the covert action requirements for pre- and post-reporting to the Intelligence Committees. As previously discussed, all intelligence activities must be reported to the SSCI and HPSCI, regardless of who performs the activity. The traditional military activities (TMA) clause is the one most often referenced by the Title 10 community to self-classify an operation as something other than an intelligence activity, thereby removing the requirement to report on it in advance through the Intelligence Committees. A significant problem with this maneuver is the disagreement between the DOD and the Intelligence Committees as to what constitutes TMA; the term is not defined in statute or in any DOD doctrinal

---

[41] Jennifer D. Kibbe, "Covert Action and the Pentagon," *Intelligence and National Security* 22, no. 1 (February 2007); Joel T. Meyer, "Supervising the Pentagon: Covert Action and Traditional Military Activities in the War on Terror," *Administrative Law Review* 59, no. 2 (Spring 2007); Vincent P. Bramble, *Covert Action Lead - Central Intelligence Agency Or Special Forces* (Leavenworth, KS: Army Command and General Staff College, 2007).

[42] 50 USC § 413b(e). The exempted activities are: "(1) activities the primary purpose of which is to acquire intelligence, traditional counterintelligence activities, traditional activities to improve or maintain the operational security of United States Government programs, or administrative activities; (2) traditional diplomatic or military activities or routine support to such activities; (3) traditional law enforcement activities conducted by United States Government law enforcement agencies or routine support to such activities; or (4) activities to provide routine support to the overt activities (other than activities described in paragraph (1), (2), or (3)) of other United States Government agencies abroad." 50 USC § 413b(e). It is interesting to note that while Congress included categories of activities that were not to be considered covert actions, it did not include a similar list outlining activities which it does consider to be covert action, adding further to the confusion.

publication. The Intelligence Committees do not appreciate what they see as anyone attempting to circumvent their oversight. Regardless of the intent behind this characterization from the Title 10 side, the Intelligence Committees often wrongly denounce the Executive Branch for attempting to avoid congressional oversight when it does so. "Wrongly" is used here because while the Intelligence Committees would not be involved in a review of the military activity in question, the Armed Services Committees of both the House and the Senate certainly would be, though the Intelligence Committees usually do not mention this fact. When they have done so, they deride their fellow members in the other committees by saying, ". . . the congressional defense committees cannot be expected to exercise oversight outside of their jurisdiction."[43] The key factors behind this misrepresentation of the oversight or lack thereof is that within Congress the same battles for power and control exist as elsewhere in the human enterprise and this area of operations suffers as a result.

The following table consolidates much of the preceding chapter into a convenient cross-reference matrix.

---

[43] House Permanent Select Committee on Intelligence, *Report to Accompany the Intelligence Authorization Act for Fiscal Year 2010*, 111th Cong., 2nd sess., 2009. H. Rept. 111-186, 49.

	Intelligence Activities		Military Activities		
	Covert Action	Not Covert Action	Intelligence Gathering	TMA	SOF Activity
Defined in Statute?	Yes	Somewhat E.O. 12333	Some	No	No (Joint Pub)
Who Authorizes?	President	Agency Heads	Depends On Type of Intel	Chain of Command	Chain of Command
Authorization Vehicle?	Finding	E.O./IAA		Order	Order/ Directive
Pre-Activity Notification Required? (to whom)	Yes SSCI/HPSCI	Preferred SSCI/HPSCI	Preferred SSCI/HPSCI	No	Yes SASC/HASC
Post-Activity Notification Required? (to whom)	Yes SSCI/HPSCI	Yes SSCI/HPSCI	Yes SSCI/HPSCI	Yes SASC/HASC	Yes SASC/HASC

This background sets the stage for a discussion on the current debate regarding cyberspace activities. Many in the cyber community are trying rightly or wrongly to cast the cyberspace discussion in the same vein as the SOF versus CIA argument while ignoring the fact that the same legal debate between Title 10 and Title 50 would necessarily be transposed over the cyberspace question as well. The next chapter addresses how the application of the SOF versus CIA template on the cyberspace argument is neither appropriate nor valid, and that cyberspace requires its own set of policies, rules, oversight, and language to function well as a tool of the U.S. government.

CHAPTER 4: THE CYBER SQUARE PEG

The previous chapter took the reader through a complex and somewhat arduous

discussion and description of the differences between covert action and military

activities. It is an old and familiar argument. The current standstill in Department of

Defense (DOD) offensive cyberspace activities (OCA) is because the Central Intelligence

Agency (CIA) asserts that OCA are covert actions, the military defines them to be

traditional military activities (TMA), and neither side is going to give up their position.

Both sides are comfortable debating and defending their positions, and both know where

the sensitive touch-points are with Congress for this sort of argument.

Why the Debate Breaks Down for Cyberspace

There are a number of problems with attempting to apply this old debate to

cyberspace. Foremost is the lack of published U.S. government (USG) policy from the

Executive Branch upon which to formulate a learned argument. As addressed in Chapter

3, there are several decades of administration policy and directed actions to fall back

upon to aid in understanding the military special operations versus CIA paramilitary or

covert actions debate. In contrast, unclassified Executive Branch policy for offensive

acts in cyberspace is intentionally soft as to be virtually non-existent[1] and directed

actions in cyberspace are only rumors by the press.[2]

---

[1] U.S. President, *National Security Strategy of the United States* (Washington, DC: The White House, 2010), 22. ". . .with tailored approaches to deterrence and ensuring the U.S. military continues to have the necessary capabilities across all domains—land, air, sea, space, and cyber." Also, U.S. President, *International Strategy for Cyberspace* (Washington, DC: The White House, 2011), 14. "When warranted, the United States will respond to hostile acts in cyberspace as we would to any other threat to our country." Classified Presidential Directives exist that address offensive cyberspace operations but which cannot be discussed in this document.

[2] Ellen Nakashima and Joby Warrick, "Stuxnet was Work of U.S. and Israeli Experts, Officials Say," *Washington Post*, 01 June 2012; Ellen Nakashima, Greg Miller, and Julie Tate, "U.S., Israel

Up until recently, there has been no U.S. law written which explicitly addresses or even mentions OCA; however, even this last is insufficiently explicit to terminate the covert action debate.[3] In the absence of actual language, both sides have been attempting to fit the proverbial square peg into a round hole of their particular choosing. This approach casually mischaracterizes many of the relevant details, running the risk that any resolution based on this misrepresentation will include a completely new series of interpretational difficulties and gray area.

One distinction is usually overlooked, namely the lack of human face-to-face interactions with an adversary in cyberspace operations. Much of the policy, law, and operating procedures for special operations or covert actions are written for a situation with boots on the ground – U.S. persons (military or civilians) would be secretively going into harm's way, might be found out, the ramifications of which could be damaging on the national or world stage. For cyberspace operations, there will be no need for the caveat "the Secretary will disavow all knowledge" of an individual, as there will be no person at risk of being physically caught or killed.[4]

Finally, there is a significant difference in how well the general operations community understands the two arenas. The conventional DOD military community at large understands the basics of special operations. They recognize the types of operations and activities as extensions of conventional operations, and they can identify the usual

---

Developed Flame Computer Virus to Slow Iranian Nuclear Efforts, Officials Say," *Washington Post*, 19 June 2012.

   [3] National Defense Authorization Act for Fiscal Year 2012, Public Law 112-81, *U.S. Statutes at Large* 125 (2011): 1551, codified at 10 USC § 111. "Congress affirms that the Department of Defense has the capability, and upon direction by the President may conduct offensive operations in cyberspace to defend our Nation, Allies and interests, subject to—

   "(1) the policy principles and legal regimes that the Department follows for kinetic capabilities, including the law of armed conflict; and

   "(2) the War Powers Resolution (50 USC 1541 et seq.)."

   [4] *Mission: Impossible*, CBS, 1966-1973.

suspects engaged in this field and respect the visible expertise special operators bring to bear. This is not the case for OCA, which is largely not understood by most of the military operations community. Offensive cyber activities are not a natural extension of basic training and "every Marine a rifleman." There are no movies or literary works to provide casual familiarity with a positive perspective for cyberspace,[5] and OCA personnel are very limited in number and their expertise has no physical component to be recognized and emulated. As such, trying to pursue a way ahead for offensive cyberspace by couching it in terms of the special operations forces (SOF) versus CIA debate is a pointless endeavor. The use of a blurry template (as discussed in Chapter 3), overlaid upon a technologically complex and embryonic domain of war further complicates attempts to understand operations in cyberspace.

Not Covert Action

The CIA's basis for their claim of covert action is that offensive activities in cyberspace are carried out such that both the activity and the sponsor (the USG) are to be undiscovered by the adversary or anyone else in the near sphere. As a declarative legal statement, this seems to be greatly lacking. The mere fact that an activity – any activity – is done secretly and anonymously does not make it a covert action. If this were the case, then the following activities must also be classified as covert actions: nearly all intelligence gathering activities of the CIA and the rest of the intelligence community (IC); many college pranks; any private investigator on a case; and others. The statutory definition of covert action only requires that the fact of U.S. involvement be hidden, as

---

[5] Compare *The Green Berets*, directed by Ray Kellogg, Batjac Productions, 1968, and *Bravo Two Zero*, directed by Tom Clegg, Distant Horizon Productions, 1999; contrast with *Swordfish*, directed by Dominic Sena, NPV Entertainment, 2001, and *Live Free or Die Hard*, directed by Len Wiseman, Twentieth Century Fox Film Corp., 2007.

was the case for many past examples of covert actions – arming revolutionaries or airdropping supplies was expected to be witnessed by whoever was in the vicinity.[6] Anonymity alone cannot define a covert action.

In all fairness to the CIA's assertion, the statutory definition of covert action includes "to influence political, economic, or military conditions abroad."[7] In the case of the previously discussed 2008-2009 alleged cyber operations against a Saudi website, one could argue that an anti-propaganda action such as taking down a website could constitute a means of affecting the political environment. However, that same argument would also mean that the CIA's alleged association with the affected Saudi website was itself a covert action; indeed, no U.S. involvement has been officially acknowledged for this activity.[8] The argument would also apply to Department of State (DOS) on-line activities, to include recent actions taken by the DOS's Center for Strategic Counterterrorism Communications to modify text on a Yemeni al-Qaeda website.[9] The DOS was not a signatory on the three-way agreement for coordination and deconfliction of cyberspace operations,[10] and in the past has expressed their disagreement via the inter-agency forum about military activities of the same sort as they carried out.[11] As with the anonymity discussion, influence alone cannot be a sole determining factor for covert action.

---

[6] For Nicaraguan Contras in the 1990s see James S. Van Wagenen, "A Review of Congressional Oversight," *Studies in Intelligence* 40, no. 5 (1997); for "Air America" see William M. Leary, "CIA Air Operations in Laos, 1955-1974," *Studies in Intelligence* 43, no. 3 (Winter 1999-2000).

[7] 50 USC § 413b(e).

[8] Ellen Nakashima, "For Cyberwarriors, Murky Terrain; Pentagon's Dismantling of Saudi-CIA Web Site Illustrates Need for Clearer Policies," *Washington Post*, 19 March 2010.

[9] Karen DeYoung and Ellen Nakashima, "U.S. Uses Yemeni Web Sites to Counter Al-Qaeda Propaganda," *Washington Post*, 23 May 2012.

[10] U.S. Department of Defense, U.S. Department of Justice, and Intelligence Community, <*Title Omitted*> (Washington, DC: Department of Defense, Department of Justice, and Intelligence Community, 2007).

[11] Nakashima, "For Cyberwarriors, Murky Terrain."

As an aside, all USG influence operations have their own separate and rigorous approval and deconfliction process across the inter-agency community of participants, to include the CIA.[12] For the DOD, this process applies to military information support operations (MISO, formerly known as psychological operations, or PsyOps) and military deception (MILDEC) activities, with approval necessary at the Secretary of Defense (SECDEF) level or higher depending on the operation. In these influence arenas, cyberspace capabilities might be a delivery mechanism for influence messages in the same way as a leaflet drop or a radio broadcast – the message itself is the influence executable that is coordinated to ensure consistency, and the delivery mechanism is of secondary consideration. Absent an effect upon cyberspace itself (deny, disrupt, degrade, or destroy), delivery activities do not constitute offensive cyber actions necessitating additional deconfliction.

Not Traditional Military Activity

The military's basis for the claim of traditional military activities in cyberspace is that the offensive actions would be carried out under a military commander (namely of U.S. Cyber Command, USCYBERCOM) in support of a military mission; in the case of the aforementioned Saudi website, it was in support of the Iraq and Afghanistan theaters.[13] The clandestine or covert nature of cyberspace activities is irrelevant to the discussion of TMA. "Military activities" is a given,[14] but attempts to couch cyberspace operations as "traditional" is a stretch. Cyber warfare is a construct of less than twenty years for the DOD, which hardly fits the definition of "traditional." Like special

---

[12] U.S. Joint Chiefs of Staff, *Information Operations*, Joint Publication 3-13 (Washington, DC: Joint Chiefs of Staff, 2012), IV-1.
[13] Nakashima, "For Cyberwarriors, Murky Terrain."
[14] U.S. Joint Chiefs of Staff, *Information Operations*, III-3.

operations, cyberspace operations require tools, tactics, techniques, and procedures that are beyond general issue. Also like special operations, authorities to execute cyberspace operations and the process to determine the appropriateness of that use should be at a level above that of conventional activities – SECDEF or higher.

It is tempting to take standing special operations doctrine and do a simple text replacement where "special operations" becomes "offensive cyberspace operations." In many ways, this is not too far off the mark. U.S. Special Operations Command (USSOCOM) and USCYBERCOM are both functional combatant commands (FCC) to which all of the armed services provide highly specialized forces and capabilities; utilization of those forces and the synchronization of actions with geographic combatant commands (GCC) is then the responsibility of the FCC vice the services. However, as will be discussed later in this chapter, the intelligence, planning, and preparation necessary for OCA usually takes a great deal more time and consumes far more resources than for special operations, in part because there is less precedent and fewer lessons learned to draw upon for examples or templates. One may use USSOCOM and SOF only loosely as a guide or aid for understanding issues and special conditions associated with the development of cyberspace operations, forces, and command and control mechanisms.

What Sort of Operations?

Combatant commands (CCMD) operate in one of two roles: as the *supported* command, wherein the CCMD has primary responsibility for a particular operation, directing or dictating any assistance it might require from others; or as a *supporting* command, wherein they provide assistance to another CCMD.[15] To apply some context to the discussion, examples follow of each of the support constructs from the perspective of USCYBERCOM with some of the different direction, coordination, and synchronization issues lightly addressed.

The Usual & Most Likely – In Support of the GCC

As previously discussed, cyberspace operations have an information operations genealogy as supporting functions to conventional kinetic campaigns. In this vein, the OCA is either replacing a kinetic action or mitigating some of the risk involved with one. For example, blocking the communications of an adversary's lookout via technical cyber methods means that he cannot report on what he sees, thereby protecting advancing friendly forces. Additionally, the ordnance that would have been used to obliterate his position may be allocated to another target. It is the job of the computer network operations (CNO) or cyber planners at the GCC and USCYBERCOM to understand what possibilities might exist for delivery of effects within the cyber infrastructure of an operating area, overlay the GCC commander's intent, and suggest possible actions for integration of cyber operations into the larger command plan. Repeated in-depth engagement with the GCC is mandatory for OCA throughout the entire development process for any contingency as a portion of a larger theater campaign plan. Regular and iterative reviews of the plan, the assessment of the strategic environment, and the intelligence understanding of the target environment are necessary to maintain a current common operating picture for possible application of offensive cyber capabilities. In the hypothetical Elbonian scenario in Chapter 2, the attack on the Kneebonian anti-air

---

[15] U.S. Joint Chiefs of Staff, *Joint Operations*, Joint Publication 3-0 (Washington, DC: Joint Chiefs of Staff, 2011), I-7.

Commodore-64 would be the supporting function providing mitigation of the risk to the pilot on his sortie. The cyber attack would require synchronization with the air mission to ensure that the outage in the Kneebonian anti-air system occurred as the flight was in progress.

There exists a significant drawback associated with the timeline of on-demand short-notice concept plan (CONPLAN) development and that is the time and resources required. It takes a great deal of time to assess the cyber environment, identify and vet targets, determine what vulnerabilities might exist, and determine what effects might be derived from any activities in cyberspace to exploit those vulnerabilities. Following these considerable tasks there is still the legal review of the operations, GCC commander's approval, and then the coordination with fires cells and effects boards for synchronization with the higher-level GCC operations before an activity executes. Cyberspace is largely not a quick-reaction capability.

The Exception – Directed Operations

USSOCOM is responsible for the Global War on Terror (GWOT) mission, wherein USSOCOM synchronizes all USG activities in the pursuit of al-Qaeda regardless of where in the world it might be necessary.[16] USCYBERCOM also has a global mission for the DOD – the synchronization and centralization of cyberspace activities and operations.[17] When SOF executes a mission upon command of the SECDEF or President, which is not part of a GCC campaign, this is a directed operation. It follows

---

[16] U.S. Special Operations Command, USSOCOM History Office, *History: United States Special Operations Command* (Tampa, FL: USSOCOM/SOCS-HO, 2008), 15. Also Eric Schmitt and Mark Mazzetti, "Secret Orders Lets U.S. Raid Al Qaeda in Many Countries," *New York Times*, 10 November 2008.
[17] U.S. Cyber Command, "United States Cyber Command," http://www.cybercom.mil/default.aspx (accessed 21 December 2012).

that USCYBERCOM could be similarly ordered to plan and execute a mission in cyberspace that is not integrated within a GCC campaign – also a directed operation. USCYBERCOM will need a GWOT-like mission under which to develop plans and tools, and pursue the technical information necessary for mission execution in advance of an actual execution order. This will be required to prioritize supporting intelligence development activities. Absent an actual execution order from the SECDEF or President, mission planning of this sort is normally done on a speculation basis that does not fare well in competition for resources against national level intelligence requirements. However, without such anticipatory development, the same timeline issues discussed earlier for on-demand CONPLAN developments apply. The following example contrasts a directed cyberspace operation from one in support of a kinetic operation.

The Elbonians have formulated a new plan to deal with the problem of the unfriendly garbage barrage: rather than a retaliatory kinetic operation, the Elbonians decide to halt the Kneebonian assault through other means. They develop STAZNOT, a computer virus designed to infect the array of Apple II computers in control of the targeting system for the Kneebonian garbage lobber. This virus will affect how the targeting system plots coordinates such that any attempt to lob garbage at Elbonia will wind up shooting straight up in the air, dropping the payload of trash on the Kneebonian garbage lobber site itself. In this situation, there is no air campaign to support and no pilot to protect – this would be a directed cyber operation.[18]

---

[18] Nakashima and Warrick, "Stuxnet was Work of U.S. and Israeli Experts."

The Elephant in the Room (*or* Does Title 10 + Title 50 = Title 60?)

The CIA is not the only Title 50 IC element with equities in cyberspace; amongst its other missions, the National Security Agency (NSA) "enables Computer Network Operations (CNO) in order to gain a decision advantage for the nation and our allies under all circumstances."[19] The language used in the strategy statement is very precise; understanding the language is necessary to understanding the NSA-USCYBERCOM partnership. In the citation, the NSA "enables" CNO: this means that the NSA applies its Title 50 intelligence expertise to assist USCYBERCOM in the planning of and preparation for potential Title 10 offensive and defensive actions in cyberspace. This potential provides national and military leadership with an operational course of action they would not have otherwise had – a "decision advantage." The NSA does not make the decision, nor would it carry out an offensive cyber mission if leadership were to decide upon that potential course of action. NSA has no offensive warfighting authorities under Title 10; execution of OCA falls to USCYBERCOM as the Title 10 organization.

OCA Cannot Happen Without CNE

The close partnership between the NSA and USCYBERCOM did not come about by chance – it was an intentional act, and crucial to the success of cyberspace operations. One of the NSA's primary missions is Signals Intelligence (SIGINT), in which the NSA "collects, processes, and disseminates intelligence information from foreign signals for

---

[19] National Security Agency, "About NSA/CSS: Strategy and Mission," http://www.nsa.gov/about/ (accessed 21 December 2012). Mission Statement: "The National Security Agency/Central Security Service (NSA/CSS) leads the U.S. Government in cryptology that encompasses both Signals Intelligence (SIGINT) and Information Assurance (IA) products and services, and enables Computer Network Operations (CNO) in order to gain a decision advantage for the Nation and our allies under all circumstances."

intelligence and counterintelligence purposes and to support military operations."[20]

Computer network exploitation (CNE) is a specialized subcategory of SIGINT:

"Enabling operations and intelligence collection capabilities conducted through the use of

computer networks to gather data from target or adversary automated information

systems or networks."[21] The military does not plan an operation without an

understanding of the operating environment, to include mission goals and end-states,

operating parameters, and detailed information on the target and terrain in which the

mission will occur. If USCYBERCOM were to plan a cyberspace operation in the

absence of highly detailed and technical information about the domain and the target, it

would be like shooting an arrow in the dark – you might hit your target or you might not,

and you might find that you are using the wrong sort of arrow. The detailed technical

information for cyberspace operational planning comes from intelligence produced by the

NSA largely via CNE, per the definition above. Knowledge of the network shapes the

operation: executing an OCA against a Commodore-64 possibly requires a different set

of tools and techniques than for an Apple II or an IBM PC.

An increased capability was achieved when the responsibilities of Commander,

USCYBERCOM met up with those of Director, NSA (DIRNSA). By conjoining the

Title 10 military operational mission authorities of USCYBERCOM with the Title 50

intelligence authorities of NSA, the result is a whole that is greater than the sum of its

two parts. The "dual-hat" at the very top of both organizations provides a consistency of

direction and prioritization of mission support to both organizations that would be

---

[20] National Security Agency, "About NSA/CSS: Strategy and Mission,"
http://www.nsa.gov/about/ (accessed 21 December 2012). Signals Intelligence Mission.
[21] U.S. Joint Chiefs of Staff, *Department of Defense Dictionary of Military and Associated Terms*,
Joint Publication 1-02 (Washington, DC: Joint Chiefs of Staff, 2010), s.v. "computer network exploitation."

virtually impossible to enact between two separate groups under different command and control lines. Indeed, many USCYBERCOM personnel currently work side-by-side with NSA employees, interacting with the same data for similar targets but in support of different missions. To ensure the professional protection of the personnel involved, the USCYBERCOM Judge Advocate and NSA General Counsel are closely involved in all activities across the two mission sets to maintain legal separation and meet all oversight and reporting requirements.

Access to the NSA expertise in CNE was the prime reason for co-locating the U.S. Strategic Command (USSTRATCOM) OCA component (then Joint Functional Component Command – Network Warfare, JFCC-NW) with the NSA in 2005, and for keeping USCYBERCOM there in 2010.[22] Contrary to oversimplified portrayals by popular media, it takes more than just one smart person and five minutes of work to hack into the mainframe of an adversary's most important computer network. The work to prepare for and execute an offensive cyberspace operation is like an iceberg. The actual Title 10 deny/disrupt/degrade/destroy function is the visible ice above the waterline; beneath the surface, 90% of the iceberg remains unseen, which is the Title 50 intelligence work necessary to prepare for a cyberspace operator to pull the virtual trigger.

Title 10 Authorities Are Not Timely Enough

As discussed, the intelligence necessary to support OCA planning and execution is difficult, time consuming, and relies upon support from intelligence organizations under different authorities than the cyber planner. Absent an assigned mission to

---

[22] In addition to CNE expertise, the NSA also has the USG mission for Information Assurance (IA). The NSA's expertise in IA and CND further supported the argument for retaining the "dual-hat" relationship when JFCC-NW merged with JTF-GNO and then became USCYBERCOM in 2010. General Alexander went "all in" by leveraging NSA authorities, workforce, and support structure to bring USCYBERCOM to an operational footing in far less time than it would have taken otherwise.

execute, the Title 10 commander is in a poor position for negotiating support from the IC. It is difficult to justify utilizing rare low-density resources in support of a planning effort that might sit on a shelf for months or years rather than expending those same resources on fulfilling national intelligence requirements. However, if the Title 10 commander must wait for an actual mission execution order to request support from cyberspace intelligence, it is entirely possible that said support would not be available in time to execute the larger mission. It is a proverbial *Catch-22* scenario.[23]

The "dual-hatted" nature of Commander, USCYBERCOM and Director, NSA (COMCYBER/DIRNSA) helps to mitigate this timing conundrum. The individual wearing both COMCYBER and DIRNSA hats, in coordination with the staffs of both USCYBERCOM and the NSA and perhaps other USG sources, may determine that intelligence development in support of an as yet undirected military operation constitutes being pro-active rather than speculative. As such, COMCYBER/DIRNSA may wield Title 50 SIGINT authorities to direct some of the intelligence collection and production necessary for the OCA planning, thereby bridging some of the gap. Upon the issuance of a Title 10 mission execution order to the supported GCC, the NSA intelligence process will already have produced information necessary for USCYBERCOM to coordinate and synchronize planning with the GCC.

Why Can USCYBERCOM Not Do It All?

In the face of all this tension between Title 10 and Title 50 and the timeliness question, it seems reasonable to ask why the tension exists at all. USCYBERCOM and the NSA are both DOD organizations; Title 10 gives the SECDEF "all authority,

---

[23] Joseph Heller, *Catch-22, A Novel* (New York, NY: Simon and Schuster, 1961).

direction, and control" over the DOD;[24] so, why has the SECDEF not directed that

USCYBERCOM do it all and avoid the Title 10 versus Title 50 debate altogether? The

answer goes back to the lines of authority for intelligence activities. The President

delegates intelligence authorities through the Director of National Intelligence (DNI) to

the heads of the IC elements, to include DIRNSA.[25] The DNI designates specific IC

heads to be functional managers for the USG for particular classes of intelligence:

Director, NSA for SIGINT; Director, CIA for HUMINT (human intelligence); Director,

National Geospatial-Intelligence Agency (NGA) for GEOINT (geospatial intelligence).[26]

The President acknowledged the fact that the NSA is a DOD organization with SECDEF

control, but limited the authority of the SECDEF to delegate SIGINT activities to other

organizations by requiring coordination with DIRNSA as the functional manager for

SIGINT.[27] While some portions of the SIGINT mission spectrum are routinely delegated

to military units for specific situations, DIRNSA has not yet done so with CNE.

Military and other DOD organizations desirous of joining the fight in cyberspace

often chafe at this restriction. They use unofficial and uncoordinated terminology to

couch their plans in what appears to be traditional military operations language. Cyber

operational preparation of the environment (C-OPE) is the latest version of this sleight of

---

[24] 10 USC § 113(b).
[25] 50 USC § 401: E.O. 12333 1.7(c)(1).
[26] 50 USC § 401: E.O. 12333 1.3(12)(A)(i)-(iii). "Functional Managers shall report to the Director concerning the execution of their duties as Functional Managers, and may be charged with developing and implementing strategic guidance, policies, and procedures for activities related to a specific intelligence discipline or set of intelligence activities; set training and tradecraft standards; and ensure coordination within and across intelligence disciplines and Intelligence Community elements and with related non-intelligence activities."
[27] 50 USC § 401: E.O. 12333 1.7(c)(2). "No other department or agency may engage in signals intelligence activities except pursuant to a delegation by the Secretary of Defense, after coordination with the Director (of the NSA)."

hand.[28] They use these arguments in an attempt to "get around the Title 50 issue" – what they want to do is traditional military OPE, and therefore must be Title 10, right?

Wrong. An individual actor or organization may not decide for themselves that their planned activity is governed by one desired set of rules or another. In cyberspace, if an activity meets the definitions and criteria codified in USC and other national security directives as signals intelligence, then that activity is subject to the rules and oversight governing execution of the signals intelligence mission regardless of who carries out the cyberspace activity or on whose behalf.[29] The "dual-hatted" nature of COMCYBER/DIRNSA places checks and balances on DOD activities in cyberspace, occasionally disappointing those attempting to manipulate the system to avoid intelligence oversight. The intentional misuse of language to obfuscate the intended mission is ineffective and calls into question the motives behind the activity. In addition, as discussed in Chapter 3, this sort of misrepresentation has been proven to raise the ire of Congressional oversight committees.

This chapter demonstrated that the existing legal and operational patterns or templates that have been misapplied to cyberspace to define activities or authorities are all inappropriate. The USG needs a new construct within which to frame cyberspace operations, including clear and concise language, authorities not in conflict or contention, and a documented and repeatable approvals process. Lastly and most importantly, cyberspace needs an oversight process that protects the United States while not hindering

---

[28] Operational preparation of the environment (OPE) has no definition listed in JP 1-02 (*DOD Dictionary*). The uncoordinated CJCS cyberspace lexicon lists "cyber-OPE," but cross-references the language to a JP 3-13 (*Information Operations*) definition of OPE which also does not exist.

[29] 50 USC § 1801 et seq. Also U.S. President, National Security Council Intelligence Directive, "Signals Intelligence," declassified copy of NSCID-6, 17 February 1972, http://www.nsa.gov/about/cryptologic_heritage/60th/interactive_timeline/Content/1970s/documents/19720 217_1970_Doc_3984040_NSCID6.pdf (accessed 24 May 2013).

the U.S. warfighter. Chapter 5 will present recommendations for one possible way

forward for cyberspace.

CHAPTER 5: RECOMMENDATIONS FOR A NEW HOLE

Chapter 1 introduced the theme or thesis statement of this document: in order to develop an effective and fully functional U.S. Cyber Command (USCYBERCOM), which includes Title 10 offensive authorities and capabilities, specific policy, legal, and legislative procedural actions must be implemented. This chapter will provide recommendations for those specific actions and will add thoughts on educating the workforce and disseminating guidance across the Department of Defense (DOD).

Executive Guidance and Policy

It all starts at the top. Executive Branch strategy documents all mention cyberspace, but largely as a security issue. As described by one author, "[t]oday's policy and legal framework for guiding and regulating the U.S. use of cyberattack is ill-formed, undeveloped, and highly uncertain."[1] Cyberspace is a new domain, and it is prudent to move forward cautiously and conscientiously. The possibility of negative results due to insufficient thought and research far outweigh the unquantifiable benefit from immediate action. However, while it is appropriate to make haste slowly, inaction has left the question too long unanswered.

In 2009, then Secretary of Defense (SECDEF) Gates exercised his authority to create USCYBERCOM. In 2010, Congress confirmed the appointment of then LTG Alexander to the four-star position of Commander, USCYBERCOM. In 2011, Congress inserted language into Title 10 to affirm military capability to carryout offensive

---

[1] William A. Owens, Kenneth W. Dam, and Herbert S. Lin, eds., *Technology, Policy, Law, and Ethics Regarding U.S. Acquisition and Use of Cyberattack Capabilities* (Washington, DC: National Academies Press, 2009), 4.

operations in cyberspace when directed by the President.[2] In spite of these tacit

acknowledgments that cyber warfare exists and that the DOD is the responsible party for

U.S. government (USG) offensive military missions in cyberspace, there are some who

still categorize cyberspace operations as covert actions. To close out the covert action

argument the administration must issue clear and incontestable guidance to all

departments and agencies of the USG. This guidance, likely in the form of an Executive

Order or Presidential Policy Directive,[3] must include language to specify that cyberspace

is a new domain and must have its own controls, deconfliction, and oversight.[4]

Additionally, it must explicitly state that the covert action construct is not appropriate for

cyberspace operations in which there are no humans in harm's way. Thus, a new set of

criteria is required to exclude cyberspace operations from covert actions as defined in

statute. Finally, in order to mitigate concerns over unexpected collateral effects and to

acknowledge the need for deconfliction with other USG actors in cyberspace, all

approvals and orders for military offensive cyberspace operations should be issued at the

SECDEF level or higher for the near term (perhaps three to five years). In this way, the

entire community is part of the process whereby the USG learns by doing, taking small

steps under restrictive control to grow a common understanding and to avoid repeating

history – namely enacting control mechanisms after an undesired situation occurs.

---

[2] National Defense Authorization Act for Fiscal Year 2012, Public Law 112-81, *U.S. Statutes at Large* 125 (2011): 1551, codified at 10 USC § 111

[3] Classified policy documents exist which address USG activities in cyberspace: U.S. President, National Security Presidential Directive, "National Strategy to Secure Cyberspace," unclassified subtitle of NSPD-38 (Washington, DC: The White House, 2004); U.S. President, Presidential Policy Directive, "U.S. Cyber Operations Policy," PPD-20 (Washington, DC: The White House, 2012). NSPD-38 included deconfliction guidance for across the USG; it has since been rescinded and replaced by PPD-20. PPD-20 is a very recent document; one may expect it to add a greater level of fidelity to Executive Branch policy direction for offensive cyberspace activities. This author has not had the opportunity to review it as of this writing.

[4] Ellen Nakashima, "Obama Signs Secret Directive to Help Thwart Cyberattacks," *Washington Post*, 14 November 2012.

The President should add one final point to the directive, suggesting terminology to separate offensive cyberspace operations from covert actions, intelligence activities, or traditional military activities. This would go a long way towards clarifying the argument in the minds of the Congressional committees that will be tasked with legislating the direction and providing the requisite oversight.

Who Gives the Order, and How Do They Do So?

USCYBERCOM, a functional combatant command (FCC), has no earth or water, no geographic area, for which it is responsible. Instead, USCYBERCOM's area of responsibility (AOR) is the global domain of cyberspace. As with geographic combatant commands (GCC), USCYBERCOM will require a steady-state plan for its AOR, one in which the Commander identifies how the command will apply military capabilities towards meeting USG desired end-states as part of the national strategy.[5] This SECDEF approved plan must include direction for shaping the cyberspace environment to avoid conflict, and preparing the USG to wage war should diplomacy and deterrence fail. In addition, the plan must include authorities to permit USCYBERCOM to do proactive development of technical capabilities and adversarial target knowledge to ensure timely response to emergent situations and the concomitant calls for support by a GCC. There must be no constraints to a theater of war or other geographic limitations.

As previously discussed, offensive cyberspace operations are not traditional military activities in the same vein as infantry or close air support. Offensive cyberspace operations must be managed and controlled at the outset in a manner similar to that of

---

[5] U.S. Secretary of Defense, *Guidance for Employment of the Force* (Washington, DC: Department of Defense, 2012). The GEF is the tasking document used by SECDEF to interpret national strategy for the Department and to identify goals or end-states for each of the combatant commands.

special access programs or other highly sensitive and restricted efforts.[6] This will not only ensure that sensitive capabilities and effects are protected but that the approvals process is managed and engaged at the highest levels.

Centralized planning and execution will be necessary in the near term to avoid negative outcomes by the "strategic corporal." Rules of engagement (ROE) for military cyberspace operations must be written, disseminated across the force, and socialized across the interagency cyber community for common understanding. These ROE must include answers to all of the usual questions (who, what, where, when, why, how) in such a manner as to always point back to USCYBERCOM and the GCC command staff for answers. Nothing may be left open to interpretation such that a brand new second lieutenant somewhere in the fray could get the idea that his or her platoon should be defacing websites or disabling Internet infrastructure.

In support of GCC operations, the planning and execution of offensive cyberspace activities will require approval from SECDEF, who will have the responsibility for notifying Congress dependent upon the effect to be achieved by the cyber capability. Setting the line between requirements for pre-operation notification versus post-operation reporting will require a great deal of negotiation and education across the oversight community. This line should change over time as the entire USG cyber community becomes better versed in the language of cyberspace, the art of the possible, the ways in which unintended effects are mitigated, and the general success of the operations being supported. For directed cyber operations not in support of a GCC, approval for planning and execution will depend upon the sensitivity of the target and the intended effect of the

---

[6] U.S. Department of Defense, *Special Access Program (SAP) Policy,* Directive 5205.07 (Washington, DC: Department of Defense, 2010). SAP is a protection system used for sensitive military development efforts, for example stealth aircraft.

operation. A Presidential finding would be an appropriate vehicle to direct the DOD to achieve a desired effect utilizing military and other capabilities. For sensitive operations, pre-operation notification to an appropriate committee of Congress should be required to affect legislated oversight.

Oversight

Congressional committees are notoriously protective of their responsibilities, whether they are statutory or merely perceived. To avoid the perception of Executive interference in Congressional oversight, the President's Order or Directive should suggest that Congress identify the appropriate oversight committee. Congress may then determine whether it prefers to use standing committees (Armed Services or Intelligence) or create a new construct altogether. In all likelihood, Congress will direct that cyberspace operations in support of a GCC plan will require some pre-operation briefing to the Armed Services committees. In keeping with past sensitivities, Congress will likely require notification of the Intelligence committees in advance of the operation for directed offensive cyberspace operations.

Deconfliction Amongst the Players

The three-way memorandum between the DOD, the Department of Justice (DOJ), and the Intelligence Community (IC) requires updating to reflect new cyberspace language and definitions.[7] It must also acknowledge the recently stated USG policy on

---

[7] U.S. Department of Defense, U.S. Department of Justice, and Intelligence Community, *<Title Omitted>* (Washington, DC: Department of Defense, Department of Justice, and Intelligence Community, 2007).

cyber attacks and the Laws of Armed Conflict.[8] The Department of State (DOS) must

become a signatory to the agreement as their recent activity on Yemeni websites has

shifted their on-line actions from strategic communications to offensive acts (the Yemeni

influence campaign actually modified data on the site).[9] Finally, the agreement must

address when and to whom a disagreement between signatories must be elevated when

one party has significant concerns and a consensus cannot be reached (as was the case

with the Saudi website incident, and the alleged resultant international relations fiasco).[10]

Legislative Requirements

Once the Executive Branch has laid out the administration's policy and guidance

for offensive cyberspace operations, Congress must then act. First, Congressional

committees will meet and make recommendations on how cyberspace activities should be

categorized and controlled, and who is responsible for the oversight within Congress

itself. Upon agreement of the oversight responsibilities, their task then is to codify it.

The challenge will be to avoid the mistakes of the past and ensure that the key

determinants and directives are included within the body of the law vice merely in

committee reports.[11]

Using a vehicle such as the annual National Defense Authorization Act or

Intelligence Authorization Act, Congress should define the exact requirements for calling

for offensive cyberspace action, for consultation with Congress in advance, and for

---

[8] Harold Koh, "International Law in Cyberspace," Opinio Juris blog, transcript posted 19 September 2012, http://opiniojuris.org/2012/09/19/harold-koh-on-international-law-in-cyberspace/ (accessed 30 September 2012).

[9] Karen DeYoung and Ellen Nakashima, "U.S. Uses Yemeni Web Sites to Counter Al-Qaeda Propaganda," *Washington Post*, 23 May 2012.

[10] Ellen Nakashima, "For Cyberwarriors, Murky Terrain; Pentagon's Dismantling of Saudi-CIA Web Site Illustrates Need for Clearer Policies," *Washington Post*, 19 March 2010.

[11] Intelligence Authorization Act for Fiscal Year 1991, Public Law 102-88, *U.S. Statutes at Large* 105 (1991): 429.

reporting to them afterwards. By using this approach, Congress brings together the House and Senate Armed Services committees, the Intelligence committees, along with the Appropriations subcommittees, thereby improving the coordination of language and interaction for cyberspace operations.[12]

Modifications to Title 10

Regardless of the vehicle Congress chooses to enact cyberspace legislation, the language will be the most important part. Under Title 10, only some clarity and specificity to the existing code is required. Legislative language will resolve the conflict by explicitly stating that the military has authority to conduct offensive cyberspace operations, regardless of type of activity or location, in support of a larger military combat operation.[13] In addition to these authorities, legislation must acknowledge that the DOD may also carry out offensive operations in cyberspace when directed to do so by Presidential writ under the authority of Commander in Chief.[14] The primary lead for any such military cyberspace operations is as per Presidential direction in the Unified Command Plan (UCP); currently, the responsibility for military cyberspace operations has been directed to U.S. Strategic Command (USSTRATCOM), who then delegated this mission to USCYBERCOM.[15]

In addition to clarifying military authority to act, Congress must also provide clear direction and guidance regarding their expectations for notification and reporting for cyberspace operations. As previously discussed, Congress might simplify their task

---

[12] Eric Lorber, "Executive Warmaking Authority and Offensive Cyber Operations: Can Existing Legislation Successfully Constrain Presidential Power?" *University of Pennsylvania Journal of Constitutional Law* XV, no. 1 (2012): 84-85.

[13] Robert Chesney, "Military-Intelligence Convergence and the Law of the Title 10 / Title 50 Debate," *Journal of National Security Law & Policy* 5, no. 2 (2012): 544.

[14] U.S. Constitution, Article 2.

[15] U.S. President, *Unified Command Plan* (Washington, DC: The White House, 2011), 28-33.

by requiring a pre-operation briefing on the cyberspace effects to be achieved in support of larger combat operations, perhaps to the combined Armed Services and Intelligence Committees. A post-operation report to both sets of committees on the performance and effectiveness of the cyberspace support will improve congressional comfort levels as well as aid in educating the larger cyber community. For directed operations, Congress should specify a process similar to that used for extremely sensitive military missions and Central Intelligence Agency (CIA) covert actions: pre-operation notification to a restricted set of senior leaders of the Armed Services and Intelligence committees.

Modifications to Title 50

Under Title 50, providing clarity and specificity to the existing code will take a bit more work than for Title 10. First, Congress must amend the covert action language sections explicitly to rule out all Title 10 offensive cyber activities. Organizations with authorities under Title 50 may still execute covert actions as directed (to include within cyberspace), though new terminology to differentiate would be very useful here.

For clarification on oversight, Congress will have more work to do. As discussed, it might be expected that Congress will specify that directed cyberspace operations require notification in advance of any operation, and the likely recipients of this notification will be the Intelligence Committees. For cyberspace, the intelligence gathering necessary for offensive action is a significant concern. Congress executes oversight of intelligence collection activities via a rigid set of processes to ensure protection of the rights and privacy of U.S. citizens. In coordination with the Director of National Intelligence (DNI), Congress must reinforce the existing oversight procedures to include those activities that must continue to be carried out by IC elements in support of military operations and thus may not be executed by the military on their own. The DNI, in consultation with the functional managers of the major intelligence categories (HUMINT, SIGINT, GEOINT), will determine what capabilities or activities might be delegated to the Title 10 planning cadre (USCYBERCOM and GCC cyber teams). In addition, they must also provide a mechanism for obtaining prioritized support from the IC for those capabilities or activities that cannot be delegated outside of the IC.

Finally, Congress must agree to language in Title 50 to provide support to the DNI and IC functional managers to carry out intelligence collection in support of military planning absent a corresponding foreign intelligence requirement. Without the freedom to prioritize developmental activities against standing national requirements, Title 10 contingency planning in cyberspace will always be starting from a time disadvantage.

Rollout Across the DOD

While Congress is addressing the language of the law, the DOD will have a larger task to resolve, that of developing and documenting cyber definitions, identifying cyber actors, and describing cyber activities for the entire department. This work will involve personnel from all levels of the DOD, including the SECDEF and staff, the Joint Chiefs of Staff (JCS), USSTRATCOM and USCYBERCOM, legal advisors from across the department, and other DOD elements as necessary to ensure the widest possible rapid acceptance and integration throughout the department.

SECDEF

The SECDEF must direct USCYBERCOM to develop the equivalent of a theater campaign plan (TCP) for steady state shape and deter activities in cyberspace. For offensive activities, the TCP must also result in a nested execution order (EXORD) similar to the Global War on Terrorism (GWOT) tasking for USSOCOM to direct USCYBERCOM to develop the capabilities and technical knowledge necessary for support to a GCC in time of crisis.

The SECDEF must work with the JCS for their guidance on clarifying the process whereby a joint force commander (at a GCC or joint task force) calls for supporting cyber fires, the division of work between USCYBERCOM personnel and the cyberspace workforce within a GCC, and the responsibilities across the board. The SECDEF will direct the JCS to develop cyberspace doctrine – in coordination across the entire DOD, to include IC elements – for the "deliberate, iterative and continuous process of planning and developing the current and future joint force."[16]

Service Doctrine

After the SECDEF directive for the creation of USCYBERCOM, several of the Services started writing and publishing cyberspace doctrine for themselves in anticipation of the formation of cyber component commands.[17] Lacking specific guidance from the Joint Staff, these doctrinal documents are currently limited in scope and detail. In future revisions, the Services must ensure that cyberspace doctrine accounts for the unique aspects of cyberspace, avoiding the temptation to take long-existing doctrine and merely replace "sea" or "air" with "cyber." The significance of the existence of service cyber doctrine is they show the Services understand that cyberspace is a field of operations that will require specific guidance, training, and information for the force.

---

[16] U.S. Joint Chiefs of Staff, "Directorate for Joint Force Development, J7," http://www.jcs.mil/page.aspx?id=22 (accessed 21 January 2013).

[17] U.S. Air Force, *Cyberspace Operations*, Air Force Doctrine Document 3-12 (Maxwell AFB, AL: Air Force, 2010); U.S. Navy, *Cyberspace Operations*, Navy Warfare Publication 3-12 (Norfolk, VA: Navy, 2011); U.S. Army, *Cyberspace Operations*, Field Manual 3-12 (Fort Eustis, VA: Army, forthcoming).

Joint Doctrine

The Joint Chiefs of Staff, working with the services and all joint force commanders, will establish the doctrine to regulate how to manage and control military cyberspace operations in a joint environment. As with service-centric doctrine, the Joint Staff must avoid falling into the trap of merely rewording existing doctrine by simply inserting "cyberspace operations" in the place of "air operations" or more likely "special operations." Similarly they must not repeat the error of the initial uncoordinated cyber lexicon, in which they chose to "align key cyberspace operations (CO) concepts with doctrinally accepted terms and definitions used in other joint operational domains" while also leaving out terminology because "they reflect missions that have no analogue in the other domains."[18]

Joint doctrine must also make clear how a joint force commander (JFC) issues a request for support via cyber means. The command relationship and the authorities and responsibilities for the planning and execution must be completely clear to all involved: it is USCYBERCOM's job to execute offensive cyberspace actions on behalf of the JFC.

Cyberspace doctrine must include guidance for all aspects of computer network operations, to include defense as well as attack. Especially for defense, this includes how cyber operators must interact and coexist with infrastructure that borders military and government networks since military and government functions are dependent upon the commercial and public cyber domain. For attack, the integration and synchronization of cyber operations will be the major challenge. Identification and tracking of targets for cyberspace action is very different from kinetic action; the type of non-physical

---

[18] U.S. Joint Chiefs of Staff, *Cyberspace Operations Lexicon* (Washington, DC: Joint Chiefs of Staff, 2010).

information necessary to deconflict and validate targets in cyberspace is beyond the current language of Joint Publication (JP) 3-60, *Joint Targeting*.[19]

Joint Publication 1-02 – the Lexicon

As an official DOD dictionary, JP 1-02 is a foundational resource for the entire military community and beyond.[20] As such, the contents of the publication must be written in clear, concise, and very specific language. Attempts to couch cyberspace terminology in terms of language from kinetic and conventional operations under the mistaken assumption that it will be easier to comprehend only induce further misunderstanding and confusion, as evidenced by the Joint Staff's first attempt at a lexicon. While the Joint Staff lexicon began the debate about cyberspace doctrine, it also resulted in the misuse of terminology not widely available to the joint force, leading many to create their own definitions and meanings for terms and adding to the friction between planners, analysts, and oversight. As a DOD resource, the definitions contained therein must be coordinated with and approved by the entire Department, not just the military. In order to create a common frame of reference for the entire USG, the lexicon should be socialized with the other USG entities with equities in cyberspace, notably the DOJ's Federal Bureau of Investigation (FBI), the DOS, and the IC. Cyberspace specific entries in the dictionary should include notations directing the reader to the appropriate JP for details, additional explanation, and examples.

---

[19] U.S. Joint Chiefs of Staff, *Joint Targeting*, Joint Publication 3-60 (Washington, DC: Joint Chiefs of Staff, 2007). JP 3-60 is currently being updated.
[20] U.S. Joint Chiefs of Staff, *Department of Defense Dictionary of Military and Associated Terms*, Joint Publication 1-02 (Washington, DC: Joint Chiefs of Staff, 2012).

As of this writing, there is no joint doctrinal publication for cyberspace. JP 3-12, *Cyberspace Operations*, currently exists as a classified draft document, the same state it has been in for several years.[21] The Joint Staff began the process of creating a doctrinal publication before the community was ready to discuss and debate the contents.

In order to draft a useful JP 3-12, the language describing cyberspace operations, especially those on the offensive end of the spectrum, needs to be extremely clear and simple. The language must reflect the lexicon included in JP 1-02, expanding upon the definitions with examples to help the reader achieve complete comprehension. For example, the current draft version of JP 3-12 uses language that is non-specific and with limited structure such that any four readers might arrive at seven different interpretations of the intent.[22]

Besides clear definitions, an effective JP 3-12 must include an extensive discussion of the authorities at work in cyberspace. In very simple non-legal terms, the document must describe the dividing lines between different mission and authority sets, to include examples of places where the lines might seem to blur, emphasizing the need to consult with subject-matter experts and legal counsel.

JP 3-12 needs to outline the various positions or job descriptions associated with cyberspace operations. This "who's who" for cyberspace will help the reader understand his/her relative position in the continuum. Position descriptions should include GCC

---

[21] U.S. Joint Chiefs of Staff, *Cyberspace Operations*, Joint Publication 3-12 (Washington, DC: Joint Chiefs of Staff, forthcoming).

[22] Ibid. Example: "Offensive cyberspace operations: OCO are CO [cyberspace operations] intended to project power by the application of force in and through cyberspace. OCO may target adversary cyberspace functions or use first-order effects in cyberspace to initiate cascading effects into the physical domains to affect weapon systems, C2 processes, critical infrastructure/key resources (CI/KR), etc."

cyber operations planner, USCYBERCOM planner at Fort Meade or with a deployed cyber support element, the cyber component commands, USCYBERCOM intelligence analysts, National Security Agency (NSA) intelligence analysts, and USCYBERCOM and NSA intelligence collection managers, at a minimum.

Most importantly, JP 3-12 needs to outline the process flow for the integration of cyberspace operations within a campaign plan. Planning is not a checklist process, and JP 3-12 is thus neither a cookbook nor stepwise how-to guide. Rather, JP 3-12 must guide the reader and planner through a number of important factors, to include any target or situational considerations, implications for or risks to execution, limitations to synchronization. Several of the JP operational series might be a good template for an effective JP 3-12; JP 3-13.1, *Electronic Warfare*, is offered as an example.[23]

The basics of JP 3-12 must be available at the unclassified level to permit widest distribution. A classified annex should be included to incorporate case studies or other situational examples as references to underscore the finer points of cyber actions and authorities to ensure the greatest possible common frame of reference for those working in the arena. This classified annex should also include a brief description of the other USG entities involved in cyberspace in some way, both within the DOD and beyond: Defense Intelligence Agency (DIA), NSA, DOJ/FBI, DOS, and CIA, to name a few. This annex might include some studies of past cyber operations where coordination went awry, further emphasizing the need for communications and deconfliction

Education & Training

Senior leadership across the DOD has cited the need to develop and retain

---

[23] U.S. Joint Chiefs of Staff, *Electronic Warfare*, Joint Publication 3-13.1 (Washington, DC: Joint Chiefs of Staff, 2007).

personnel with the skills and knowledge necessary for USG cyberspace operations, both

defensive and offensive. The Department's *Strategy for Operating in Cyberspace* states

> The development and retention of an exceptional cyber workforce is
> central to DOD's strategic success in cyberspace and each of the strategic
> initiatives outlined in this strategy. . .The development of the cyber
> workforce is of paramount importance to DOD.[24]

However, the *Strategy* goes into no further detail on how the DOD will do that for

military development. The development of a cadre of "cyber warriors" will require both

training and education. The Services are making some advances in the training and

education of their service members on cyberspace, but this is being done independently.

Service training and education needs to be carried out in coordination with and under the

direction of USCYBERCOM to ensure consistency and commonality as a lead-in for

future joint cyber training.

Creating Cyber Warriors – the Pipeline

Early identification of aptitude will be critical for new cyber recruits. Men and

women entering the military today have grown up with cyberspace as an integral part of

their lives. Language will not be the problem so much as an understanding of the

restrictions imposed by the rule of law. Those with the aptitude for highly technical

cyber skill fields must be directed towards advanced schooling after completion of basic

training and A-level schools. The Services spend a lot of time training their personnel in

how to configure and maintain networks and computer systems; there must be equal time

spent educating the troubleshooters and the outside-the-box thinkers.

The Joint Network Attack Course (JNAC) and Joint Cyber Analysis Course

---

[24] U.S. Department of Defense, *Department of Defense Strategy for Operating in Cyberspace* (Washington, DC: Department of Defense, 2011), 10.

(JCAC) need to be expanded in capacity immediately.[25] Both courses should be

available to junior level officers and enlisted as entry-level familiarity to a career in

computer network operations (CNO), as well as the more senior personnel who are

shifting into CNO from another skill field.

For personnel inbound to USCYBERCOM or to one of its service components in

a planner billet, JNAC and the CNO Planner's Course (see below) must be mandatory

training en route. For those heading towards an analyst billet at USCYBERCOM, JCAC

must be an additional requirement. For personnel headed to a GCC on a CNO billet, the

CNO Planner's Course should be a minimum requirement with JNAC at first availability.

NSA must expand its digital network intelligence training programs for better

support to USCYBERCOM. This training curriculum must be mandatory to anyone

filling a CNO analyst billet at USCYBERCOM or one of its service components. This

would apply to both offensive and defensive positions, as the analysis of network

metadata is a key component part of both missions.

CNO Planners Course

The Army's 1st Information Operations Command runs the Basic CNO Planners

Course (BCNOPC), which is a mere ten days in length and Army-centric in nature. This

provides students with a minimum exposure to the cyberspace arena but no depth of

understanding; when they report for duty, they will have heard the words but will not be

able to explain what any of it means or apply any of the principles of cyber operations.

This course must be extended in breadth and depth to graduate students with a better than

---

[25] All Partners Access Network, "IO Course Catalog - Joint Network Attack Course," http://wss.apan.org/1753/Lists/IO%20Course%20Catalog/DispForm.aspx?ID=107 (accessed 21 January 2013); All Partners Access Network, "IO Course Catalog - Joint Cyber Analysis Course," http://wss.apan.org/1753/Lists/IO%20Course%20Catalog/DispForm.aspx?ID=4 (accessed 21 January 2013).

basic understanding of all of the issues and considerations that must be taken into account when the option of a cyberspace activity is debated. [26] An alternative way ahead would be to use the BCNOPC as the basis for a new and significantly more detailed joint course to prepare members from all of the Services for duty at USCYBERCOM or a GCC.

As discussed above, this new expanded course must become mandatory education for anyone en route to an assignment as a cyber planner or cyber analyst. It is recommended education for anyone working in adjunct or supporting positions at USCYBERCOM, its components, or any other tangential cyber position across the enterprise. It would behoove the DOD to run this program at two different levels: one for junior personnel who will be cyber professionals for a large part of their careers; and one for mid-level personnel who have been assigned to a cyber-related staff position or are cross training to another career field.

This education will provide the students with a common language, an understanding of the authorities, and knowledge of the various USG entities engaged in activities in cyberspace. This education should be aided by case studies and hypothetical scenarios to put the information into perspective and show the applicability of different issues to the situation, and must include the planning criteria, desired effects, choice of capability and how it was executed, success or failure of the operation, any collateral effects, and battle damage assessments.

CAPSTONE

Despite the recent increasing emphasis on cyberspace as a warfighting domain, it

---

[26] U.S. Army, Intelligence and Security Command, 1st Information Operations Command, "IO Training Overview – Basic Computer Network Operations Planners Course," http://www.1stiocmd.army.mil/Home/iotraining (accessed 18 January 2013).

is not yet well understood by many operational commanders and senior leaders. A lack of knowledge as to the full capabilities and limitations of cyberspace has increased the amount of risk commanders accept when cyberspace is involved in their operation, and many are ignorant that they are doing so.

In addition to training and education for personnel who will be doing the bulk of the day-to-day work in cyberspace operations planning, there is also a need to ensure that senior leadership is sufficiently conversant in the language and issues of cyberspace in order to provide their guidance and make their decisions from a position of knowledge. The CAPSTONE program for general officer training would offer a venue for providing basic (or even remedial) training about cyberspace.[27] Using the Executive CNO Planners Seminar (ECNOPS) offered by the 1st IO Command, new senior leaders would be provided with an exposure to the language, authorities, constraints and restraints, policies, command relationships, and other information necessary for them to be successful.[28] The ECNOPS should be augmented with real world case studies to put all of the above into context.

The steps outlined in this chapter provide the policy, legal, and educational framework necessary for successful USG military cyberspace operations. A whole of government deconfliction requirement was identified and a mechanism for conflict

---

[27] National Defense University, "CAPSTONE," http://www.ndu.edu/CAPSTONE/ (accessed 31 January 2013). "The CAPSTONE curriculum examines major issues affecting national security decision making, military strategy, joint/combined doctrine, interoperability, and key allied nation issues."

[28] U.S. Army, Intelligence and Security Command, 1st Information Operations Command, "IO Training Overview – Executive Computer Network Operations Planners Seminar (ECNOPS)," http://www.1stiocmd.army.mil/Home/iotraining (accessed 21 January 2013). "The Executive Computer Network Operations Planners Seminar (ECNOPS) is an 8-hour seminar which provides a strategic/operational level introduction to CNO and cyberspace planning. The target audience for the ECNOPS is general/flag officers and their senior staff members. The topics covered in the ECNOPS include cyber lexicon, authorities, guidance, organizations, command relationships, processes for integration into military planning, cyber policy, and related current operations."

resolution was suggested. Finally, guidance was provided for Congressional actions to clarify and codify their authorities and oversight responsibilities for offensive cyberspace activities.

CONCLUSION

As stated at the outset of this discussion, the U.S. joint force commander is currently limited in his or her ability to utilize cyberspace capabilities to achieve his or her mission. This limitation is not technical in nature; rather it is based in the politics of power and control.

Resolution of this limitation is being debated and argued using a construct and terminology from a well-trodden though highly inappropriate scenario about special operations versus paramilitary action. The misapplication of the scenario by both sides of the debate, which adds to the frustration felt by all of the participants, does nothing to end the gridlock in cyberspace. Those in positions to provide guidance and clarity to the debate have failed to do so.

Herein are identified a series of linked actions necessary to provide the policy, legal, operational doctrine framework for USG military cyberspace operations. As of this writing, the policy direction has been lightly addressed in a way that supports U.S. military offensive cyberspace operations but does not completely end the covert action argument; fully voiced support may exist in a classified form. It is up to Congress to incorporate their direction within the U.S. Code to guide the operational constraints for the joint force commander. Finally, the Department of Defense must write clear language and doctrine for the joint force, and significantly expand and enhance the education and training of cyberspace personnel to meet the specialized needs of this new domain of war.

An eminently workable solution exists for ending the current standstill. Achieving access to the full spectrum of cyberspace capabilities for the joint force commander, to include offensive cyber activities in support of conventional military operations, is readily doable. The only obstacle in the way of forward movement on this topic is the political will to do so, and the all too usual battles for power and control that occur within a government bureaucracy.

BIBLIOGRAPHY

Books, Journals, and Papers

Alexander, Keith B. "Warfighting in Cyberspace." *Joint Force Quarterly: JFQ* 46 (3rd Quarter 2007): 58-61.

Andrues, Wesley R. "What U.S. Cyber Command Must Do." *Joint Force Quarterly: JFQ* 59 (4th Quarter 2010): 115-120.

Belk, Robert and Matthew Noyes. *On the Use of Offensive Cyber Capabilities: A Policy Analysis on Offensive US Cyber Policy.* Cambridge, MA: John F Kennedy School of Government, 2012.

Berger, Joseph B. III. "Covert Action: Title 10, Title 50, and the Chain of Command." *Joint Force Quarterly: JFQ* 67 (4th Quarter 2012): 32-39.

Birdwell, M. Bodine and Robert Mills. "War Fighting in Cyberspace: Evolving Force Presentation and Command and Control." *Air & Space Power Journal* 25, no. 1 (2011): 26-36.

Bradbury, Steven G. "The Developing Legal Framework for Defensive and Offensive Cyber Operations." *Harvard National Security Journal* 2, no. 2 (2011): 591-612.

Bramble, Vincent P. *Covert Action Lead -- Central Intelligence Agency Or Special Forces.* Leavenworth, KS: Army Command and General Staff College, 2007.

Cahanin, Steven E. *Principles of War for Cyberspace.* Maxwell AFB, AL: Air War College, 2011.

Carter, Rosemary M., Brent Feick, and Roy C. Undersander. "Offensive Cyber for the Joint Force Commander: It's Not that Different." *Joint Force Quarterly: JFQ* 66 (3rd Quarter 2012): 22-27.

Chesney, Robert. "Military-Intelligence Convergence and the Law of the Title 10 / Title 50 Debate." *Journal of National Security Law & Policy* 5, no. 2 (2012): 539-629.

Cogan, Charles G. "Covert Action and Congressional Oversight: A Deontology." *Studies in Conflict and Terrorism* 16 (1993): 87-97.

Crowell, Richard M. *War in the Information Age: A Primer for Cyberspace Operations in 21st Century Warfare.* Newport, RI: Naval War College, 2012.

Dycus, Stephen. "Congress's Role in Cyber Warfare." *Journal of National Security Law & Policy* 4, no. 1 (2010): 155-171.

Engelmann, Bettina and Paula Cordaro. *Cyber Commander's Handbook: The Weaponry & Strategies of Digital Conflict.* McMurray, PA: Technolytics Institute, 2010.

Farwell, James P. and Rafal Rohozinski. "The New Reality of Cyber War." *Survival* 54, no. 4 (September 2012): 107-120.

Gervais, Michael. *Cyber Attacks and the Laws of War*. New Haven, CT: Yale University School of Law, 2011.

Graham, David. "Cyber Threats and the Law of War." *Journal of National Security Law & Policy* 4, no. 1 (2010): 87-102.

Grant, Rebecca. *Rise of Cyber War*. Washington, DC: Mitchell Institute for Airpower Studies, 2008.

Gross, Richard C. *Different Worlds: Unacknowledged Special Operations and Covert Action*. Carlisle, PA: Army War College, 2009.

Heller, Joseph. *Catch-22, A Novel*. New York, NY: Simon and Schuster, 1961.

Huntley, Todd C. "Controlling the Use of Force in Cyber Space: The Application of the Law of Armed Conflict During a Time of Fundamental Change in the Nature of Warfare." *The Naval Law Review* 60 (2010): 1-40.

Jensen, Eric T. "Computer Attacks on Critical National Infrastructure: A Use of Force Invoking the Right of Self-Defense." *Stanford Journal of International Law* 38 (Summer 2002): 207-240.

Johnson, Loch K. "The Church Committee Investigation of 1975 and the Evolution of Modern Intelligence Accountability." *Intelligence & National Security* 23, no. 2 (April 2008): 198-225.

Kibbe, Jennifer D. "Conducting Shadow Wars." *Journal of National Security Law & Policy* 5, no. 3 (2012): 373-392.

———. "Covert Action and the Pentagon." *Intelligence and National Security* 22, no. 1 (February 2007): 57-74.

Kramer, Franklin D., Stuart H. Starr, and Larry K. Wentz, eds. *Cyberpower and National Security*. Dulles, VA: Potomac Books, 2009.

Leary, William M. "CIA Air Operations in Laos, 1955-1974." *Studies in Intelligence* 43, no. 3 (Winter 1999-2000): 71-86.

Libicki, Martin C. *Cyberdeterrence and Cyberwar*. Washington, DC: RAND Corporation, 2009.

———. "Cyberspace is Not a Warfighting Domain." *I/S: A Journal of Law and Policy for the Information Society* 8, no. 2 (2012): 321-336.

Lin, Herbert. "Offensive Cyber Operations and the Use of Force." *Journal of National Security Law & Policy* 4, no. 1 (2010): 63-86.

Lorber, Eric. "Executive Warmaking Authority and Offensive Cyber Operations: Can Existing Legislation Successfully Constrain Presidential Power?" *University of Pennsylvania Journal of Constitutional Law* 15 (forthcoming): 1-85.

Mahoney, John R. *Reflections on a Strategic Vision for Computer Network Operations.* Carlisle, PA: Army War College, 2010.

Meyer, Joel T. "Supervising the Pentagon: Covert Action and Traditional Military Activities in the War on Terror." *Administrative Law Review* 59, no. 2 (Spring 2007): 463-478.

Mudrinich, Erik M. "Cyber 3.0: The Department of Defense Strategy for Operating in Cyberspace and the Attribution Problem." *Air Force Law Review* 68 (2012): 167-206.

Mustin, Jeff and Harvey Rishikof. "Projecting Force in the 21st Century - Legitimacy and the Rule of Law: Title 50, Title 10, Title 18, and Art. 75." *Rutgers Law Review* 63, no. 4 (Summer 2011): 1235-1251.

Owens, William A., Kenneth W. Dam, and Herbert S. Lin, eds. *Technology, Policy, Law, and Ethics Regarding U.S. Acquisition and Use of Cyberattack Capabilities.* Washington, DC: National Academies Press, 2009.

Radsan, A. John. "An Overt Turn on Covert Action." *Saint Louis University Law Journal* 53, no. 2 (Winter 2009): 485-552.

Rattray, Gregory and Jason Healey. *Categorizing and Understanding Offensive Cyber Capabilities and Their Use.* Washington, DC: National Academies Press, 2010.

Sharp, Walter Gary Sr. *Cyberspace and the Use of Force.* Falls Church, VA: Aegis Research Corporation, 1999.

———. "The Past, Present, and Future of Cybersecurity." *Journal of National Security Law & Policy* 4, no. 1 (2010): 13-26.

Shulman, Mark R. "Discrimination in the Laws of Information Warfare." *Columbia Journal of Transnational Law* 37, no. 3 (1999): 939-968.

Smart, Steven J. "Joint Targeting in Cyberspace." *Air & Space Power Journal* 25, no. 4 (2011): 65-75.

Snider, L. Britt and Center for the Study of Intelligence. *The Agency and the Hill: CIA's Relationship with Congress, 1946-2004.* Washington, DC: Center for the Study of Intelligence, 2008.

Strange, Joseph L. and Richard Iron. "Center of Gravity: What Clausewitz Really Meant." *Joint Force Quarterly: JFQ* 35 (October 2004): 20-27.

Strange, Joe. "Centers of Gravity & Critical Vulnerabilities: Building on the Clausewitzian Foundation So That We Can All Speak the Same Language." *Perspectives on Warfighting* 4, 2nd ed. (1996): 1-152.

U.S. Special Operations Command. USSOCOM History Office. *History: United States Special Operations Command.* Tampa, FL: USSOCOM/SOCS-HO, 2008.

Waddell, William. *Cyberspace Operations: What Senior Leaders Need to Know About Cyberspace.* Carlisle, PA: Army War College, 2011.

Walker, Paul A. *Traditional Military Activities in Cyberspace: Preparing for "Netwar."* Berkeley, CA: ExpressO, 2010.

Wall, Andru E. "Demystifying the Title 10-Title 50 Debate: Distinguishing Military Operations, Intelligence Activities & Covert Action." *Harvard National Security Journal* 3, no. 1 (September 2011): 85-142.

Waxman, Matthew C. "Cyber-Attacks and the Use of Force: Back to the Future of Article 2(4)." *The Yale Journal of International Law* 36, no. 2 (2011): 421-459.

Williams, Brett T. "Ten Propositions Regarding Cyberspace Operations." *Joint Force Quarterly: JFQ* 61 (2nd Quarter 2011): 11-17.

Wingfield, Thomas C. *The Law of Information Conflict: National Security Law in Cyberspace.* Falls Church, VA: Aegis Research Corporation, 2000.

Van Wagenen, James S. "A Review of Congressional Oversight." *Studies in Intelligence* 40, no. 5 (1997): 97-102.

Governmental Reports and Bills

Congressional Research Service. *Congressional Oversight of Intelligence: Current Structure and Alternatives*, RL32525. Washington, DC: Congressional Research Service, 2012.

———. *Covert Action: Legislative Background and Possible Policy Questions*, RL33715. Washington, DC: Congressional Research Service, 2011.

———. *"Gang of Four" Congressional Intelligence Notifications*, R40698. Washington, DC: Congressional Research Service, 2012.

———. *Intelligence Authorization Legislation: Status and Challenges*, R40240. Washington, DC: Congressional Research Service, 2012.

———. *Presidential Directives: Background and Overview*, 98-611. Washington, DC: Congressional Research Service, 2008.

———. *Sensitive Covert Action Notifications: Oversight Options for Congress*, R40691. Washington, DC: Congressional Research Service, 2012.

———. *Special Operations Forces (SOF) and CIA Paramilitary Operations: Issues for Congress*, RS22017. Washington, DC: Congressional Research Service, 2009.

———. *U.S. Special Operations Forces (SOF): Background and Issues for Congress*, RS21048. Washington, DC: Congressional Research Service, 2012.

National Commission on Terrorist Attacks upon the United States. *The 9/11 Commission Report: Final Report of the National Commission on Terrorist Attacks upon the United States*. New York, NY: Norton, 2004.

U.S. Congress. House. "Strengthening and Enhancing Cybersecurity by using Research, Education, Information, and Technology Act of 2012 (H.R. 4263)." *Congressional Record* 112th Cong., 2nd sess. (27 March 2012): H1641.

U.S. Congress. House. Permanent Select Committee on Intelligence. *Report to Accompany Intelligence Authorization Act for Fiscal Year 2010*. 111th Cong., 2nd sess., 2009. H.Rept. 111-186.

U.S. Congress. Senate. "Cyber Intelligence Sharing and Protection Act (H.R. 3523.RFS)." *Congressional Record* 112th Cong., 2nd sess. (7 May 2012): S2920.

U.S. Department of Defense. *Cyber Operations Personnel Report: Report to the Congressional Defense Committees as Required by Public Law 111-84*. Washington, DC: Department of Defense, 2011.

———. *Cyberspace Policy Report: A Report to Congress Pursuant to the National Defense Authorization Act for Fiscal Year 2011, Section 934*. Washington, DC: Department of Defense, 2011.

———. *Quadrennial Defense Review Report*. Washington, DC: Department of Defense, 2010.

U.S. Strategies and Guidance

U.S. Department of Defense. *Department of Defense Strategy for Operating in Cyberspace*. Washington, DC: Department of Defense, 2011.

U.S. Department of Defense and U.S. Department of Homeland Security. *Memorandum of Agreement between the Department of Homeland Security and the Department of Defense Regarding Cybersecurity*. Washington, DC: Department of Defense and Department of Homeland Security, 2010.

U.S. Department of Defense, U.S. Department of Justice, and Intelligence Community. *<Title Omitted>*. Washington, DC: Department of Defense, Department of Justice, and Intelligence Community, 2007.

U.S. Department of State. *The United Nations Conference on International Organizations. San Francisco, California, April 25 to June 26, 1945: Selected Documents*. Washington, DC: Government Printing Office, 1946.

U.S. Joint Chiefs of Staff. *The National Military Strategy of the United States of America*. Washington, DC: Joint Chiefs of Staff, 2011.

U.S. President. *Comprehensive National Cybersecurity Initiative - Unclassified Synopsis*. Washington, DC: The White House, 2010.

———. *International Strategy for Cyberspace*. Washington, DC: The White House, 2011.

———. *Memorandum of Disapproval for the Intelligence Authorization Act, Fiscal Year 1991*. College Station, TX: George Bush Presidential Library and Museum, 1990. http://bushlibrary.tamu.edu/research/public_papers.php?id=2520&year=1990&month=11 (accessed 19 January 2013).

———. *National Security Strategy of the United States*. Washington, DC: The White House, 2010.

———. *Unified Command Plan*. Washington, DC: The White House, 2011.

———. Homeland Security Presidential Directive. "Critical Infrastructure Identification, Prioritization, and Protection." HSPD-7. Washington, DC: The White House, 2003.

———. National Security Council Intelligence Directive. "Signals Intelligence." Declassified copy of NSCID-6, 17 February 1972. http://www.nsa.gov/about/cryptologic_heritage/60th/interactive_timeline/Content/1970s/documents/19720217_1970_Doc_3984040_NSCID6.pdf (accessed 24 May 2013).

———. National Security Decision Directive. "Approval and Review of Special Activities." Declassified extract from NSDD-286. http://www.reagan.utexas.edu/archives/reference/Scanned NSDDS/NSDD286.pdf (accessed 14 January 2013).

———. National Security Presidential Directive. "National Strategy to Secure Cyberspace." Unclassified subtitle of NSPD-38. Washington, DC: The White House, 2004.

———. Presidential Decision Directive. "Critical Infrastructure Protection." PDD-63. Washington, DC: The White House, 1998.

———. Presidential Policy Directive. "U.S. Cyber Operations Policy." PPD-20. Washington, DC: The White House, 2012.

U.S. Secretary of Defense. *Establishment of a Subordinate Unified U.S. Cyber Command Under U.S. Strategic Command for Military Cyberspace Operations*. Washington, DC: Department of Defense, 2009.

———. *Guidance for Employment of the Force.* Washington, DC: Department of Defense, 2012.

———. *National Defense Strategy of the United States.* Washington, DC: Department of Defense, 2008.

———. *Sustaining U.S. Global Leadership: Priorities for 21st Century Defense.* Washington, DC: Department of Defense, 2012.

Doctrinal Publications

U.S. Air Force. *Cyberspace Operations,* Air Force Doctrine Document 3-12. Maxwell AFB, AL: Air Force, 2010.

U.S. Army. *Cyberspace Operations*, Field Manual 3-12. Fort Eustis, VA: Army, forthcoming.

U.S. Department of Defense. *Special Access Program (SAP) Policy,* Directive 5205.07. Washington, DC: Department of Defense, 2010.

U.S. Joint Chiefs of Staff. *Cyberspace Operations,* Joint Publication 3-12. Washington, DC: Joint Chiefs of Staff, forthcoming.

———. *Cyberspace Operations Lexicon.* Washington, DC: Joint Chiefs of Staff, 2010.

———. *Department of Defense Dictionary of Military and Associated Terms*, Joint Publication 1-02. Washington, DC: Joint Chiefs of Staff, 2010.

———. *Electronic Warfare,* Joint Publication 3-13.1. Washington, DC: Joint Chiefs of Staff, 2007.

———. *Information Operations,* Joint Publication 3-13. Washington, DC: Joint Chiefs of Staff, 2012.

———. *Joint Operations,* Joint Publication 3-0. Washington, DC: Joint Chiefs of Staff, 2011.

———. *Joint Targeting*, Joint Publication 3-60. Washington, DC: Joint Chiefs of Staff, 2007.

———. *Special Operations,* Joint Publication 3-05. Washington, DC: Joint Chiefs of Staff, 2011.

U.S. Navy. *Cyberspace Operations*, Navy Warfare Publication 3-12. Norfolk, VA: Navy, 2011.

Speeches, Hearings, Transcripts, and Interviews

International Committee of the Red Cross. "31st International Conference of the Red Cross and Red Crescent: International Humanitarian Law and the Challenges of Contemporary Armed Conflicts; 28 November – 01 December 2011." Geneva, CH: ICRC, 2011.

Koh, Harold. *"International Law in Cyberspace."* Opinio Juris Blog. Transcript posted 19 September 2012. http://opiniojuris.org/2012/09/19/harold-koh-on-international-law-in-cyberspace/ (accessed 30 September 2012).

O'Connell, MaryEllen and Louise Arimatsu. "Meeting Summary: Cyber Security and International Law." London, UK: Chatham House, 29 May 2012.

Panetta, Leon. Interview by Jim Lehrer, *PBS Newshour*, under ""CIA Chief Panetta: Obama made 'Gutsy' Decision on Bin Laden Raid," Transcript of PBS News Hour Interview of 03 May 2011." PBS. http://www.pbs.org/newshour/bb/terrorism/jan-june11/panetta_05-03.html (accessed 14 December 2012).

U.S. Congress. House. Armed Services Committee. *U.S. Cyber Command: Organizing for Cyberspace Operations.* 111th Cong., 2nd sess., 23 September 2010.

U.S. Congress. Senate. Armed Services Committee. *Posture Statement of Admiral William H. McRaven, USN, Commander, United States Special Operations Command.* 112th Cong., 2nd sess., 06 March 2012.

U.S. Congress. Senate. Select Committee on Intelligence. *Nomination of General Michael V. Hayden, USAF, to be Director of the Central Intelligence Agency.* 109th Cong., 2nd sess., 18 May 2006.

Magazine Articles (print and online)

"U.S. Short on Offensive-Mission Cyber Experts." *Federal Times*, 09 July 2012.

"Marching Off to Cyberwar." *The Economist Technology Quarterly*, Q4 2008.

Alexander, Keith B. "Mission Success in Cyberspace." *Military Information Technology*, July 2010.

Alfred, Randy. "May 21, 1901: Connecticut Sets First Speed Limit at 12 MPH." *Wired.Com*, 21 May 2008. http://www.wired.com/science/discoveries/news/2008/05/dayintech_0521 (accessed 02 January 2013).

Berinato, Scott. "Calculated Risk: Return on Security Investment." *CSO: Security and Risk*, 09 December 2002. http://www.csoonline.com/article/217727/calculated-risk-return-on-security-investment (accessed 18 January 2013).

Clayton, Mark. "'Cyber Pearl Harbor': Could Future Cyberattack Really be that Devastating?" *The Christian Science Monitor*, 07 December 2012.

http://www.csmonitor.com/USA/2012/1207/Cyber-Pearl-Harbor-Could-future-cyberattack-really-be-that-devastating (accessed 12 January 2013).

Cowley, Stacy. "Former FBI Cyber Cop Worries about a Digital 9/11." *CNN Money*, 25 July 2012. http://money.cnn.com/2012/07/25/technology/blackhat-shawn-henry/index.htm (accessed 12 January 2013).

Engleman, Eric and Michael Riley. "Political Gridlock Leaves U.S. Facing Cyber Pearl Harbor." *Bloomberg*, 15 November 2012.

GMA News. "Teenage Hackers Arrested for Hit on UK Police's Anti-Terror Hotline." *GMA News Online*, 15 April 2012. http://www.gmanetwork.com/news/story/255022/scitech/technology/teenage-hackers-arrested-for-hit-on-uk-police-s-anti-terror-hotline (accessed 2 January 2013).

Goldman, David. "Major Banks Hit with Biggest Cyberattacks in History." *CNN Money*, 28 September 2012. http://money.cnn.com/2012/09/27/technology/bank-cyberattacks/index.html (accessed 18 January 2013).

Hodges, Cynthia. "United States Official Warned of 'Cyber 9/11' Threat." *Examiner.Com*, 03 December 2012. http://www.examiner.com/article/united-states-officials-warned-of-cyber-9-11-threat (accessed 12 January 2013).

Honan, Mat. "Cosmo, the Hacker 'God' Who Fell to Earth." *Wired*, 11 September 2012.

Lin-Liu, Jen. "Huawei-Cisco Tests China's Respect for Property Rights." *IEEE Spectrum*, August 2003.

Lynn, William J. III. "Defending a New Domain: The Pentagon's Cyberstrategy." *Foreign Affairs*, September/October 2010.

Magnuson, Stew. "Defense Department Partners with Industry to Stem Staggering Cybertheft Losses." *National Defense*, December 2011.

————. "Do Cyberwarriors Belong at Special Operations Command?" *National Defense,* August 2011.

Nimmo, Kurt. "Former CIA Official Predicts Cyber 9/11." *Infowars*, 04 August 2011. http://www.infowars.com/former-cia-official-predicts-cyber-911/ (accessed 12 January 2013).

Takaheshi, Dean. "Intellectual Property Theft Fuels Underground Cyber Economy." *Venture Beat*, 27 March 2011. http://venturebeat.com/2011/03/27/intellectual-property-theft-fuels-the-underground-cyber-economy/ (accessed 18 January 2013).

Violino, Bob. "How to Stop Your Executive from being Harpooned." *Infoworld*, 23 May 2011. http://www.infoworld.com/d/security/how-stop-your-executives-being-harpooned-946 (accessed 18 January 2013).

Yoskowitz, Andre. "Teenage Hacker Arrested for Hitting 259 Websites." *AfterDawn News*, 20 April 2012.
http://www.afterdawn.com/news/article.cfm/2012/04/20/teenage_hacker_arrested_fo r_hitting_259_websites (accessed 2 January 2013).

<u>Online Resources</u>

All Partners Access Network. "IO Course Catalog - Joint Network Attack Course."
http://wss.apan.org/1753/Lists/IO%20Course%20Catalog/DispForm.aspx?ID=107 (accessed 21 January 2013).

———. "IO Course Catalog – Joint Cyber Analysis Course."
http://wss.apan.org/1753/Lists/IO%20Course%20Catalog/DispForm.aspx?ID=4 (accessed 21 January 2013).

Book, Betsy. "Virtual Worlds Review."
http://www.virtualworldsreview.com/info/whatis.shtml (accessed 31 December 2012).

Federal Bureau of Investigation. "What we Investigate - Cyber Crime."
http://www.fbi.gov/about-us/investigate/cyber (accessed 21 December 2012).

Gromov, Gregory. "Roads and Crossroads of the Internet History."
http://www.netvalley.com/history_of_internet.html (accessed 31 December 2012).

National Defense University. "CAPSTONE." http://www.ndu.edu/CAPSTONE/ (accessed 31 January 2013).

National Security Agency. "About NSA/CSS: Strategy and Mission."
http://www.nsa.gov/about/ (accessed 21 December 2012).

U.S. Army. Intelligence and Security Command. 1st Information Operations Command. "Basic Computer Network Operations Planners Course."
http://www.1stiocmd.army.mil/Home/iotraining (accessed 21 January 2013).

———. "Executive Computer Network Operations Planners Seminar."
http://www.1stiocmd.army.mil/Home/iotraining (accessed 21 January 2013).

U.S. Cyber Command. "United States Cyber Command."
http://www.cybercom.mil/default.aspx (accessed 21 December 2012).

U.S. Department of Defense. "Biography of Leon E. Panetta, Secretary of Defense."
http://www.defense.gov/bios/biographydetail.aspx?biographyid=310 (accessed 14 December 2012).

U.S. Joint Chiefs of Staff. "Directorate for Joint Force Development, J7."
http://www.jcs.mil/page.aspx?id=22 (accessed 21 January 2013).

U.S. Special Operations Command. "United States Special Operations Command." http://www.socom.mil/default.aspx (accessed 21 December 2012).

U.S. Strategic Command. "United States Strategic Command." http://www.stratcom.mil/ (accessed 21 December 2012).

Newspapers

Bumiller, Elisabeth and Thom Shanker. "Panetta Warns of Dire Threat of Cyberattack on U.S." *New York Times*, 11 October 2012.

DeYoung, Karen and Ellen Nakashima. "U.S. Hacks Web Sites of al-Qaeda Affiliate in Yemen." *Washington Post*, 24 May 2012.

Hersh, Seymour M. "C.I.A. Admits Domestic Acts, Denies 'Massive' Illegality." *New York Times*, 16 January 1975.

———. "Huge C.I.A. Operation Reported in U.S. Against Antiwar Forces, Other Dissidents in Nixon Years." *New York Times*, 22 December 1974.

———. "Underground for the C.I.A. in New York: An Ex-Agent Tells of Spying on Students." *New York Times*, 29 December 1974.

Nakashima, Ellen. "Cyberweapons on Pentagon Fast Track." *Washington Post*, 10 April 2012.

———. "Defense Dept. Develops List of Cyber-Weapons." *Washington Post*, 01 June 2011.

———. "For Cyberwarriors, Murky Terrain; Pentagon's Dismantling of Saudi-CIA Web Site Illustrates Need for Clearer Policies." *Washington Post*, 19 March 2010.

———. "New Cyber Command Chief Warns of Possible Attacks; U.S. Military Networks in War Zones could be Targeted, Alexander Says." *Washington Post*, 04 June 2010.

———. "Obama Signs Secret Directive to Help Thwart Cyberattacks." *Washington Post*, 14 November 2012.

———. "Pentagon is Debating Cyber-Attacks." *Washington Post*, 06 November 2010.

———. "Pentagon Officials had Weighed Cyberattack on Gaddafi's Air Defenses." *Washington Post*, 18 October 2011.

———. "U.S. Accelerating Cyberweapon Research." *Washington Post*, 18 March 2012.

Nakashima, Ellen and Brian Krebs. "As Cyberattacks Increase, U.S. Faces Shortage of Security Talent." *Washington Post*, 23 December 2009.

Nakashima, Ellen, Greg Miller, and Julie Tate. "U.S., Israel Developed Flame Computer Virus to Slow Iranian Nuclear Efforts, Officials Say." *Washington Post*, 19 June 2012.

Nakashima, Ellen and Joby Warrick. "Stuxnet was Work of U.S. and Israeli Experts, Officials Say." *Washington Post*, 01 June 2012.

Schmitt, Eric and Mark Mazzetti. "Secret Orders Lets U.S. Raid Al Qaeda in Many Countries." *New York Times*, 10 November 2008.

www.ingramcontent.com/pod-product-compliance
Lightning Source LLC
Chambersburg PA
CBHW080315290526
45790CB00005B/2053